Juggling Your Bipolar Life

Juggling Your Bipolar Life

◆

New, Successful Ways of Treating and Dealing With Bipolar Disorder

Learning to Juggle Bipolar Disorder

Choose your thoughts and think positively

Christine Schloder

iUniverse, Inc.
New York Lincoln Shanghai

Juggling Your Bipolar Life
New, Successful Ways of Treating and Dealing With Bipolar Disorder

iUniverse books may be ordered through booksellers or by contacting:

iUniverse
2021 Pine Lake Road, Suite 100
Lincoln, NE 68512
www.iuniverse.com
1-800-Authors (1-800-288-4677)

SHEP Programs
Self-Help Educational Prevention-Ed. Programs
Providing self-help educational servers since 1995
cmschloder@yahoo.com
http://bipolardisordershepp.tripod.com

Photographs by Dean Erich
Erich's Photo Barn Studio
Dean Erich67@yahoo.com
Weedville PA 814-787-4016

ISBN-13: 978-0-595-37771-8 (pbk)
ISBN-13: 978-0-595-82147-1 (ebk)
ISBN-10: 0-595-37771-8 (pbk)
ISBN-10: 0-595-82147-2 (ebk)

Printed in the United States of America

A special thanks to Randi Tyler for helping me with the spelling and editing process of this book. Her help was greatly appreciated.

Contents

Introduction

I have been bipolar for thirty-eight years, but I was only diagnosed three years ago. I struggled with the disorder for many years until I learned to cope. To be able to gain balance in my life, I focused on learning everything I could about bipolar disorder. It is my hope that this book will help all those who are seeking the same balance I so desperately needed years ago.

The best way to begin dealing with bipolar disorder is to learn as much as possible about the illness. Only with up-to-date information can you learn the most effective treatment methods. With that in mind, this book aims to help those with bipolar disorder by doing the following:

1. Helping you learn the most up-to-date treatment methods for bipolar disorder

2. Helping you understand bipolar disorder

3. Helping you understand its symptoms

4. Showing you how to make your own symptoms chart

5. Helping you learn effective methods of management and recovery

6. Showing you how to address personal issues related to bipolar disorder through a plan of action

7. Showing how to cope with crisis by change and adaptation

8. Helping you change the way you think about and deal with problems

If you suffer from bipolar disorder, you should never think it will simply go away. You must prepare yourself for it, and train yourself to do the things that will minimize its most devastating effects. When the National Institute of Mental Health began research on bipolar disorder, they quickly learned that the manic phase of the illness was often lightened by creativity, energy, and an upward spike in intelligence. Also, bipolarity seems to be more often found in the most visible members of society: artists, leaders, and performers.

Typically, once the manic energy is spent, a person plummets into the depths of depression. The mind may slow to such a degree that even the smallest decisions become impossible dilemmas. Often it seems that life is no longer worth living, but with proper diagnosis and treatment, those afflicted with bipolar disorder can lead meaningful lives.

1

For fifteen years, I was what I would call a "good manic." I had no idea that I had bipolar disorder; it just was what I was. I cleaned my house all the time. I worked in my yard and took care of the kids; everything had to be just perfect. I never stopped working until I went to bed. I slept very little. I would awaken during the night, wax the kitchen floor, wash the walls, and dust. I was a "neat freak." I could not stand the sight of dishes in my sink or things on the floor. Everything had its place. The instant anything was moved, I knew, and immediately put it back. It was an obsession.

I involved myself in various committees and organizations. I could not just be a committee member. I was so deeply involved in whatever I was doing that it would become my life. This was the manic in me.

I would work on whatever it was, night and day, until it was completed. I described myself as a workaholic to others. My goal was to get things done. I wanted to make things better for the organizations. I was so focused on making things happen that I often ended up stepping on toes without even knowing it. I was just trying to help. People got mad, but I didn't know why. Only later did I understand.

I was thirty-two years old and doing far too much. I was a single mom trying to raise two children. I had started a self-help program called SHEPP (Self-Help Educational Prevention-Ed Programs). I was traveling all over the state doing SHEP programs—sometimes five assembly programs in a day. I was also a professional juggler. I spent a lot of time going to meetings and doing juggling shows. I traveled across the United States. I wrote, produced, and performed a self-help video called "What About Self-Esteem?" I used puppets, ventriloquism, and juggling to educate young people. I was full of energy. Researching, performing, and traveling while being a single mother: this was my life.

Then I lost all my energy. I was seldom even motivated to leave my house. I withdrew from friends and family. I was not able to keep up with day-to-day tasks. I went from doctor to doctor, trying to find out what was wrong with me. When they told me I was depressed, I felt embarrassed. I tried to hide my symptoms from those around me. It didn't work. I was hospitalized. They treated my depression with many medications, but nothing seemed to work. My depression continued. I had difficulty getting out of bed each day, and was even having trouble focusing on my family's needs. It wasn't until a year later that my doctor discussed bipolar disorder with me. It was then that I was able to see the manic behaviors I had prior to becoming depressed. Looking back, I could see periods of ups and downs throughout my life. The symptoms became very apparent.

The doctors knew what it was, but no one knew how to treat it properly. Treatments were based on trial and error. Medications, therapy, and many more hospitalizations ensued. I would find relief in medications, but I continued to experience frequent cycles of illness-related thoughts and behaviors. The little progress I would make often came with side effects: anxiety, dizziness, aches and pains, and sleepiness. It was difficult to determine which were symptoms of bipolar disorder and which were side effects of the medication. It was very frustrating. I was referred to Dickinson Mental Health Center for follow-up psychiatric care. I was assigned an intensive case manager named Bobbianne O'Dell, who coordinated all my outpatient care. I'd had several doctors and outpatient therapists before, but I hadn't felt comfortable with them. Not so with Bobbianne. I found my relationship with her to be beneficial.

I started keeping a daily checklist. My case manager and I developed a list of my symptoms. As I began to experience some relief from them, I was better able to acknowledge what my symptoms were. It wasn't until a manifestation would go away that I realized it was related to my illness. My checklist grew to over forty identifying criteria. On some days, I would go through it several times; on other days only once. With time, I was better able to determine when I needed to use the checklist and when I didn't need it. When I felt my symptoms returning, I would turn back to my checklist. This helped me gauge the severity of my illness and figure out when it was time to seek help, or possibly inpatient care.

Bipolar disorder became my new obsession. As my illness improved, I set myself to learning as much as possible about it. I wanted to be able to maintain my level of stability. I began my own research. I kept notes and was able to learn what worked for me. I went from doctor to doctor until I found one who was willing to work with me. His name was Dr. Scott Turkin, MD. His practice was in DuBois, Pennsylvania Behavioral Health Center.

Dr. Turkin set me up with Mark Stoltz as my therapist. They worked with me for over a year, trying to help me get my life in order and my illness under control. Together, they gave me the best help I ever received. They really cared about what happened to me. Later, I was asked to join a bipolar research program headed by Dr. Turkin at DRMC (DuBois Regional Medical Center). This gave me even more insight into my illness. I was assigned a new therapist named Sherry Murphy. I was also able to keep my other therapist, Mark Stoltz. I spent two to three days a week taking tests and talking with my therapist and doctor. This may sound like too much, but it taught me how to handle my manic and depressed times. A crisis plan was developed for me. I had contact numbers and a support system. After a few months, I cut back to weekly, and eventually, bi-weekly visits. During periods when my symptoms worsened, they would see me more often. We worked together as a team to get me whatever level of care I needed. I was always able to reach one of them in times of crisis. About six months later, my daughter Jessica and I were asked to take part in another bipolar study at Western Psychiatric Clinic in Pittsburgh.

With medication, talk therapy, and a positive outlook and lifestyle, I am better able to keep my illness in balance. Having found success in ways to lessen the effects of my illness, I decided to put it all in a book, to help others who are suffering from bipolar disorder. I condensed all my information into one small book for easier reading, and so you can have a hand-held guide to balancing your bipolar life.

Andrea Fagiolini's Book Review

Andrea Fagiolini's comment about "Juggling Your Bipolar Life."

I am an assistant professor of psychiatry at the University of Pittsburgh School of Medicine and the medical director of the study at the Bipolar Disorder Center for Pennsylvanians.

This is an interesting, useful, and pleasant-to-read book, with an abundance of useful information for patients with bipolar disorder and their families. The author correctly points to the importance of tracking the changes in symptoms and affective states as a way to take control over the bipolar disorder and improve its course and its prognosis. The medication and symptoms tracking charts that are presented in the book are very useful aids to accomplish this goal. Also, they are an excellent way to track (and then report to the treating therapist and psychiatrist) the symptom fluctuations between one visit and another.

From a Therapist's Perspective

As a therapist, it has been my privilege to be a part of Christine's journey in learning to not only cope, but also thrive while having the diagnosis of bipolar disorder. Many people often say that their best help comes from one who knows what it is like to walk in their shoes. Christine has walked mile after mile in the shoes of bipolar disorder, and I appreciate her self-disclosure and honesty, and the practical information offered in the book. She in no way sugar-coats her struggles, but she also offers tangible evidence that one does not have to be controlled by this illness. She truly helps the reader to understand what it is like to live with bipolar disorder. Her balanced, practical, and personal approach offers hope to the reader.

Christine is living proof that every person is unique. I have personally been inspired to see Christine work through the highs and the lows of her illness and come up with a workable management plan. If you, like Christine, have been diagnosed with bipolar disorder, please know that you are much more than a bipolar person. Instead, like Christine, you are a special and unique individual, with your own talents and purpose in life. My belief is that this book can be one tool in helping you on the journey of becoming who you are meant to be.

—Mark Stoltz, LCSW

Another Therapist Offers a Point of View on Bipolar Disorder

Bipolar disorder has many "faces," meaning that symptoms differ from patient to patient, and that each individual can present in a different manner. A symptoms list in a typical DSM (Diagnostic and Statistic Manual of Disorders) book or other diagnostic book is merely a guideline. I have seen individuals who become overspenders while in a manic phase, and others who become very functional and productive and accomplish a multitude of daily tasks in a relatively short period of time. Others' emotions become very irate, with peaks of agitation. Yet others experience no manic features at all, but display more depressive symptoms.

I have known Christine for over eight years. Having worked in the mental-health field for over ten years, the most prominent thing that comes to mind when working with a bipolar individual is acceptance. A bipolar individual often does not consider her/his manic episodes as symptoms. This is a direct result of feeling great, having bursts of energy, getting things accomplished, and doing fun things. Acceptance of one's symptoms is the key to getting the correct treatment. Often misdiagnosed, bipolar disorder is commonly mistreated as depression. I have found that until accepting that manic episodes are part of the bipolar diagnosis and not part of "feeling normal," treatment efforts become limited.

One of the key ways Christine gathers information about her symptoms is the use of her daily charting system. This was a key in helping her to identify correlations between her daily activities and sleep patterns, as well as precursors to her "episodes." As she monitored all these things intently on a daily basis, she became more able to adapt to the changes in her moods—her highs and lows—because she was able to anticipate the feelings that were coming next. She also was able to curtail the length of her episodes by seeking immediate treatment, extra visits, and medication changes sooner, so as to alleviate the intensity of her symptoms. I would encourage the reader to study the charting system presented in this book. Include any and every activity or change in daily routine in your chart. Personalize your chart to include your symptoms. This may help lead to a greater awareness of how exactly your life is affected by your bipolar disorder.

Knowing Christine has given me an amazing outlook and an increased respect for individuals with bipolar disorder. To struggle day to day with changes in emotions, mood swings, and uncontrollable levels of energy takes great courage and strength—greater than one can ever imagine. It has helped to put my life into perspective a great deal. I think about my day planners, my schedules, my appointments, and my lists of things I plan to accomplish in upcoming days. Then I imagine them being torn to shreds. This is what it is like for an individual suffering from bipolar disorder. All the plans, all the intentions, all the appointments…all put on hold. If you suffer from bipolar disorder, take great pride in knowing there is help, there is hope, and there is life! Good luck!

Dr. Scott Turkin's Perspective

I have been a psychiatrist for over a decade, and my interest in the brain and its disorders precedes that by many years. For over two years now, I've had the pleasure of being the principal site investigator in DuBois, Pennsylvania of a large and several-year study called the Bipolar Disorder Center for Pennsylvanians (BDCP), centered at the University of Pittsburgh. The principal investigators are David Kupfer, MD and Ellen Frank, PhD, and the medical director for the study is Andrea Fagiolini, MD. All are very well-known experts in this field. We have enrolled over a hundred patients in our site and are deep into the second year of monitoring their progress.

It is with great satisfaction that I can assist my patient, Christine Schloder, in her quest to share her story of struggle and recovery, in the hope it can be both educational and inspirational for others. I think the key aspects of optimal management of this illness can be divided into what I call the three "rights": right diagnosis, right treatment, and right attitude and behavior.

Right Diagnosis

From surveys, we know that it is commonplace for the correct diagnosis of bipolar disorder to lag the onset of symptoms by several years. The reasons are multiple and varied, but certainly include some combination of denial and stigma regarding psychiatric conditions, under-recognition by the medical community, lack of access to specialists in many areas, and the difficulty inherent in the diagnosis itself, as people usually present with depressive symptoms alone. It is very important that professionals, advocates, and those who suffer from bipolar disorder work together to improve recognition and access, since we have evidence that early treatment not only can alleviate current suffering, but can also improve the long-term course of the illness.

Right Treatment

It is very important to find the appropriate professionals who can provide state-of-the-art treatment. This ideally includes a psychiatrist, and often a licensed counselor or therapist with experience in this disorder. Contact a local university, a professional society, or your family doctor for a referral. It's very important that you feel you can build a trusting relationship with your care providers; this will be a long-term relationship. Treatment includes both medication and psychotherapy. The latter takes various forms of both group and individual therapies.

Some psychotherapies of proven value are cognitive-behavioral therapy (CBT) and interpersonal and social rhythm therapy (IPSRT), developed by Dr. Ellen Frank and colleagues at the University of Pittsburgh. There is good evidence for the benefit of family interventions as well.

Right Attitude and Behavior

Use the self-help strategies you learn from whatever sources and adhere to the treatment regimen you develop with your doctor. This may include, among many things, great caution in using non-prescribed mood-altering substances, regularity in daily routines, regular exercise, sound nutrition, and good sleep hygiene. It means keeping appointments and being actively engaged in your care. Ask questions, and be sure you understand what is known about this illness; recognize and accept that more remains to be learned. It means struggling against stigma from others as well as any such attitudes you may have internalized yourself. Seek out the best care available and fully utilize it. Remember that this is a chronic, serious illness for which no cure is available, but that with the three "rights," it is manageable, and full functioning is always the goal. Never forget that while this illness impacts many aspects of your life, it is only one part of a unique and complex human being—you!

Tri-County Sunday News

Research Study on Bipolar Disorder Being Conducted in Philadelphia and in DuBois, PA
Joann Seltzer

A research study on bipolar disorder is close to home for people in the tri-county area. Dr. Scott Turkin, the medical director for behavioral health services at DuBois Regional Medical Center and the clinical assistant professor of psychiatry for the University of the Pittsburgh School of Medicine, is involved with a research study on bipolar disorder with the Bipolar Center for Pennsylvania. The multi-year study began at the Western Psychiatry Institute of the University of Pittsburgh Medical Center.

Studies are being conducted in both Philadelphia and DuBois. "It's a great opportunity to be able to work with the top people in our field and be part of the study," Turkin said. Bipolar disorder is a chronic brain disease that includes periods of abnormal elation or irritable moods, changes in sleep patterns and activity, talkativeness, and at other times, depression and feelings of worthlessness or guilt, he said. The condition has had a clinical name for centuries, but it had previously been called manic-depressive disorder. The clinical name was changed in the 1980s to bipolar disorder. The disorder is characterized by ups and downs. Since everyone experiences ups and downs in moods, it's the length of these periods that can help lead to a diagnosis. By definition, a person with bipolar disorder type one will remain in a manic state for at least a week, or it could be much longer, Turkin said. A person with type one of this disorder who is in the manic state may possibly have hallucinations or delusions with them. A person with bipolar disorder two has less severe symptoms, there are no hallucinations, and the manic period will last at least four days, but the amount of time a person may remain in this state is still being debated, Turkin said. The periods of depression for both types of bipolar disorder last for at least two weeks longer than the periods of mania. The clinical diagnosis of this disorder often includes information from other people who know the patients, since a person with bipolar disorder who is in the depressive state may minimize the highs, making it difficult to diagnose it, Turkin said. The clinical diagnosis also requires eliminating other possible causes, such as drugs, alcohol, or a medical condition that may result in similar highs and lows. Family members or the patients themselves are often the first to notice there is an issue. Symptoms of major depression can be almost identical to bipolar disorder for a person in the depressive state, but the distinction is made because people with bipolar disorder have had at least one manic period, Turkin said. The disorder does not discriminate; both men and women are affected equally, and usually the symptoms become noticeable in late teens or early adulthood. It can also appear in children, though it's harder to diagnose and there is more controversy. A person with a relative who has the disorder is more likely to have it, although it's possible to have it without another family member having it. The triggers for a bipolar episode can start with a major stress or loss, although as more episodes occur, fewer triggers are necessary. People in the manic state can be extremely creative and very productive people, as long as the manic state is not so severe that the person becomes disorganized, he said. People in the manic state can be little grandiose; they think highly of themselves and get a lot done. "They can have a lot of energy and can be infectious to be around," Turkin said. Sometimes they can also go too far. Not all people in the manic state get euphoric highs; some people become irritable and can make other people angry, Turkin said. The biggest challenges people with bipolar disorder have are getting the right diagnosis, struggling to accept the diagnosis once it is made, and finding the right treatment. The disorder can cause terrible suffering and be very disruptive, making it hard to stay in relationships or keep jobs, and can even lead to trouble with the law. The suicide rate is also very elevated among people with this disorder. The main treatments that are available are medication and counseling. The medication helps a patient to deal with the psychological problems that can crop up and it's helpful, but the medication to stabilize moods is a necessary component, Turkin said. The therapy helps patients to focus on the early warning signs before it goes too far. Traditionally, it was thought that about one percent of the population had bipolar disorder, but now most studies say it's more frequent and it would be safe to say that as much as three percent of the population has it, Turkin said. This is the second year DRMC has been involved in the research study. The study actually began three years ago and will last a total of four years. The hospital's participation in the study will likely lead to other studies with UPMC (University of Pittsburgh Medical Center)

2

About Bipolar Disorder

Bipolar disorder is an illness that causes disturbances in feelings, thoughts, and behavior. People who have this disorder experience episodes of low mood (depression) that alternate with periods of extremely high mood and energy (mania). The word "bipolar" refers to the way moods shift back and forth between two extremes, or poles. These intense and often sudden mood swings may seriously interfere with your ability to function, and can disrupt your relationships with family and friends. This condition is sometimes called manic-depressive illness or manic depression.

Bipolar disorder is different from major depression, which causes prolonged episodes of low mood. These episodes are often followed by gradual return to normal, or more often, are helped through treatment. More than one in a hundred people in the United States—nearly three million in all—suffer from bipolar disorder. Men and women are affected equally. The condition most commonly appears for the first time when people are in their early twenties, although anyone from adolescents to the elderly can be affected. In many cases, the intense shifts in mood can recur several times over the course of months or years. Some people, however, may experience long periods of normal mood and behavior between episodes. Usually bipolar disorder is first diagnosed during a manic episode, although people may have suffered with earlier depressions that had gone unrecognized. A manic episode is commonly preceded or followed by a depressive episode, although sometimes people have two or more periods of depression before experiencing mania.

The Cause of Bipolar Disorder is Unknown

Researchers believe that mood disorders are the result of physical changes in the brain; they're not sure what causes these changes. Because many people with this disorder have relatives who also suffer from mood disorders, inherited factors may be involved.

Stress May Trigger Bipolar Illness

Episodes of depression or mania may arise during times of stress, but the illness will sometimes return without any apparent trigger. While experiencing mood swings, a bipolar person may do things that can lead to trouble. During mania, for example, one might feel wildly energetic and powerful. One might spend all one's money, start complicated projects, or become flirtatious and promiscuous. When depressed, one might grow isolated from friends or activities and think about or attempt suicide. The stress that results from decisions made or actions taken while experiencing a mood swing can be so severe that it aggravates the illness.

Definitions of Bipolar Disorder

I obtained most of this information from a variety of psychology books and by talking with many doctors. I truly believe that as research continues on the definitions, they will in time change to a certain degree. Be sure to talk to your doctor to determine what type of bipolar disorder you have; the psychological definitions of bipolar disorder are complex.

Bipolar One Disorder: The occurrence of one or more manic or mixed episodes (both manic and major depressive episodes) for at least a week is the defining feature of bipolar one disorder. Often the person has had one or more major depressive episodes.

Bipolar Two Disorder: Defining characteristics of bipolar two disorder are one or more major depressive episodes and at least one hypomanic episode that may or may not be accompanied by depressive episodes. Diagnosis depends on the current episode. A person may sometimes cycle between manic and depressed states in what is called "rapid cycling." Moods may fluctuate between manic and depressed states, with periods of normal mood in between.

Bipolar Disorder Not Otherwise Specified: The bipolar disorder is not characteristic of any other types of bipolar disorder mentioned. The experiences of bipolar disorder vary from person to person. Occasionally someone will experience the symptoms of a manic episode and a major depressive episode, but not fit into the above mentioned types of bipolar disorder.

Cyclothymic Disorder: This is a chronic fluctuating mood disturbance involving periods of hypomanic symptoms and periods of depressive symptoms. It is a milder form of bipolar disorder. The periods of both depressive and hypomanic symptoms are shorter and less severe, and do not occur with regularity.

Hypomanic Episode: This is similar to a manic episode, except that delusions or hallucinations are not present. Also, a person's mood during an episode must be clearly different from the individual's usual non-depressed mood, with a change in functioning. The change is observable by others, but not severe enough to cause marked impairment in social or occupational functioning, or to necessitate hospitalization.

Manic Episode: This is a distinct period of persistently elevated, expansive, or irritable mood, lasting at least one week. During this period, three or more symptoms of mania must be present (see "Signs and Symptoms"). Insight and judgment are poor in the manic phase. The person may engage in excessive activities such as gambling or spending sprees and wild or excessive sexual activity. The mood disturbance is acute enough to adversely impact occupational functioning, normal social activities, or relationships, and may necessitate hospitalization to prevent harm to the patient or others. There may be psychotic symptoms.

Major Depressive Episode: When five or more symptoms of depression (see "Symptoms" page) are present during the same two-week period, and at least one of the symptoms is depressed mood or loss of interest or pleasure, it is called a major depressive episode.
When symptoms of a manic episode and a major depressive episode are both present every day for at least a one-week period. It is also called a major depressive episode.

Rapid Cycling: This is defined as having four or more manic, mixed, or hypomanic episodes in a one-month period. Either a period of partial or full remission for at least two months or a switch to an episode of opposite polarity marks these episodes.

Triggers (Stressors): Triggers are any actions, mental or physical, that start reactions (the loss of a job, a death in the family, an argument with a friend).

Environment: Your environment plays a large role in your illness and recovery. What else is going on in your life? What else might you need to work on? What are your stressors? Are there other problems that need to be addressed—family problems, personal relationships, money, drugs, or alcohol?

Obsession: Those of us with bipolar disorder need to be wary of becoming obsessed, since obsession is a characteristic of our illness. It can have both positive and negative outcomes.

Being obsessive—spending too much time being extremely organized and focused—certainly speeds the mastery of skills in any new area of growth. In excess, obsession can lead to a successful career at the cost of participation in family life. Too frequently, the end result is a wrecked marriage and family. People in this situation may be left wondering if their success was worth it. When limits have not been set and you get fixated on a goal, the price you pay to attain that goal may be too high. Anyone can fall victim to this. You must set limits and take time for other things in your life.

Myths about Bipolar Disorder

When it comes to mental illness, most people fear what they do not understand. Here are some myths that you may have heard:

Myth: People with bipolar disorder almost always commit suicide.
Truth: It is true that suicide is more common among people with bipolar disorder than people with many other mental conditions, but not everyone with bipolar disorder commits suicide. Sometimes a person experiencing a manic episode stops taking his medication because he wants to enjoy the high. Unfortunately, without proper medication, he can potentially suffer more severe suicidal impulses.

Myth: People diagnosed with bipolar disorder spend their lives in mental institutions.
Truth: Bipolar disorder is a common illness that is experienced by millions of people. The vast majority of sufferers receive treatment outside of a hospital. Only in the event of an

extreme manic or severe depressive episode are some people admitted to a hospital for their own safety. Mental institutions generally are reserved for those whose illness is so severe that they are unable to take care of themselves. With appropriate treatment, many people with bipolar disorder live normal lives.

Myth: People with bipolar disorder can't hold down jobs.
Truth: Bipolar disorder, like other mood disorders, does not entirely take away a person's ability to function. It does affect people's moods in such a way that they may feel like they cannot do something, even though they are able to.

3

My Life as a Reference Point

These next few pages are a brief summary of my life from childhood to the present. This is just to give you an idea of where I came from and what I went through to get where I am today.

Christine's Childhood Years

As a first-grader, I struggled with a learning disability. I also had a rare eye disorder: cataracts in both eyes. A cataract is a film that covers the lens of your eye, making it hard to see. It gets thicker as you get older. In 1972, it was unheard of for a child to have cataracts. It was known as a disease that only affected the elderly. My Catholic school would not accept the fact that I had cataracts. The principal and my teacher told me that I was lazy and stupid.

My third-grade teacher got mad at me because I could not read, so she went over to the first-grade class and brought a little boy back to our classroom. She made him stand in front of me and read as she told the class, "Look how dumb Christine is. A first-grader can read, and she can't." I felt embarrassed and confused about why I was unable to read. I asked to go the restroom, but instead I left the school and walked home. My self-esteem was at an all-time low. I told my mom what had happened. She said she was going to enroll me in the public school.

I was feeling very sad and hopeless. I just wanted to die. I felt there was nothing to live for. I went out to my backyard and got a rope. I climbed a big tree, tied one end of the rope around my neck, tied the other to a branch, and jumped. The branch broke, and I fell to the ground. I lay there for a while, the wind knocked out of me. I had no sooner gotten the rope off my neck than my mom came out. I told her I fell out of the tree. This was just my first suicide attempt.

I was out of school for three weeks before my mom placed me in the public school. They had a special-education teacher work with me. My self-esteem was so low that I had no motivation to learn.

When I was in fifth grade, a neighborhood teenager noticed that I was depressed. She gave me some marijuana to help me feel better. This was something new to me. It took me away from my problems and gave me a feeling of comfort. By the time I was twelve, I was doing drugs and drinking.

In sixth grade, I learned to juggle. It was the only thing I could do well. I started doing shows for local fairs. Juggling was all I had to keep me going. I was struggling in school, and I could not see well, so how was I going to learn to read? I truly thought I was dumb. I couldn't read, which made it hard for me to do any of my schoolwork.

I was very angry with myself for being dumb. I began physically abusing myself by making small cuts on my arms with a knife. It was a way to relieve all of the anger I felt. When someone asked me what had happened, I would tell them it was from briar bushes.

I became known for helping kids who were being bullied. Most of the kids I helped were smart. I asked for their help with my class work. We would not sign the top of our worksheets, and when my friend was done, she would drop her paper on the floor. I would then pick it up, put my name on it, and hand it in as mine. This is how I got through school.

I learned to read in the ninth grade, thanks to one particular teacher who cared. She understood why I was having a difficult time with my class work. She could see that I had missed the early building blocks of reading and spelling. I spelled words as they sounded. That was the best I could do. On her own time, she would stay after school with me and teach me how to read.

4

Teen Years

I abused drugs and alcohol from age eleven to fifteen, and I made many more suicide attempts. One attempt almost ended my life. I took a bunch of pills and went to my friend's house, where I passed out. I was taken to the hospital by ambulance. It looked as if I was not going to make it. The doctor told my mom that if I did make it, I would probably have brain damage. They called a priest. He read me my last rites. I learned later that I let out a scream, then came to for a few minutes.

I was put on a ventilator in the intensive care unit (ICU). I had tubes everywhere. I lay unconscious for three days. On the third day, I awoke and felt a drop of water on my face, I looked, and my youngest sister, Amy, was standing over me, crying. I looked around, and my whole family was there. I could not speak because of the tubes. I thought, *What the hell is their problem?* I was full of anger, because I had survived. I just wanted to die.

Later that day, they moved me to a private room, where they kept me for two weeks. The hospital had someone stay with me around the clock. Back then, there was no place to put a kid like me. No one knew what to do with me. There just wasn't any hope in my life. I felt I had nothing to live for. I made a few more attempts to end my life, and I was put in an adult psychiatric unit. This just kept me from partying. I had been partying a lot. Drinking eased my pain. I didn't know it at the time, but I was self-medicating.

I tried speed and found I needed to take twice the amount other kids did in order to get high. I used it two or three times a day. It would make me feel normal. I would use it before school. With it, I found I could sit still and even concentrate. I was ready to learn. I wanted to take in all that knowledge, but I found I could not put it on paper. My mind had all these

17

thoughts and ideas, and I could not get them out. The only things I really excelled at were hands-on projects, like my juggling. It was all I had. When I was doing shows, I never drank or did drugs. It was the only thing that kept me out of trouble.

At a young age, I learned from my dad how to do wiring and electrical work. It came to me naturally, but I was too busy partying to use my talent. I was a tomboy—a risk-taker all the way. (A feature of bipolar disorder is recklessness and risk taking.) I would drive my three-wheeler up a big hill that no one else would even try. I would climb tall trees just because someone said I couldn't do it. Over the years, I had many broken bones and sprains. My family thought I was accident-prone. By the age of fifteen, I had been in an adult psychiatric unit four times. I would get out and go right back to partying again. I needed to ease my pain. I felt so out of control and mixed up, and I didn't know how to deal with these feelings.

To add to all my problems, an older man took advantage of me and raped me. This was the last straw. I hit rock bottom and I was planning to end my life. I got a lot of pills together and ran away to the woods. I walked the railroad tracks for a long time. I felt numb. I kept walking until I ended up in the next town. That's where the adult unit was. I thought I would try one more time to get help. I walked in and admitted myself. I made up my mind to quit all drugs and to try to get better.

The hospital felt they could not help me, so I was sent away to an adolescent psychiatric hospital for ninety days. The first week was hell. The withdrawal made me sick. I lay in bed for two weeks. I could not eat, and I couldn't stop shaking. I was cold and hot all at once. The staff told me that if I did not start eating, I was going to have to be fed intravenously. I got better, with time. I kept my room very neat, and got lots of points on the point system; this allowed me to do fun things with the staff. I got my life back on the right track. I set goals. I was going to go back to doing juggling shows, and I was going to race my three-wheeler when I got out. By age sixteen, I was what I would call a "good manic" (hypomanic). That lasted fifteen years, to age thirty-one.

I was very creative in everything I did. I was a professional juggler, doing shows all over the USA and Canada. The shows were a mix of comedy and juggling. I also spent a lot of time in the woods, riding my three-wheeler with my friends. We would go out in a big field and do trick riding. We stayed in a cabin we had built ourselves. It was our own little world. I also got to race my three-wheeler. My first race was against all guys, and I won. Some of the guys took it pretty hard.

I dated a guy named Chris off and on for seven years. I thought I was in love with him, but when I got pregnant, he was not happy about it. I was several months along and showing when he dumped me. I had a friend named Bill who used to go riding with me. He had liked me for as long as I could remember. He said he would marry me and take care of the baby and me. We got married when I was eight months pregnant, and three days later, Bill left for the army.

My daughter Sheena was born when I was nineteen. Then Bill came home. That was when I realized I had married for all the wrong reasons. I found myself in an abusive marriage for nine years. At the time, I believed this was normal. I spent those years being the best mom I could be. I cleaned my home all the time; I was a "neat freak," and I could not sit still.

By the time I was twenty-one, there was surgery available to remove cataracts. I got my eyes fixed. I could see! I was ready to learn how to spell, but Bill was holding me back. Because of his abusive nature, I was afraid to leave Sheena home alone with him. When Bill got drunk, he would hurt me and say things like, "You can have Chris's baby, but you can't have mine." He kept throwing away my birth-control pills. He demanded that I have his baby. The situation worsened. He would come home and violently rape me. He once beat me for three days straight. As a result of the rapes, I became pregnant.

At age twenty-two, I had my daughter Jessica. It was obvious from day one that she had a problem. She cried all the time, and she never took naps. She would get out of her crib and get into things. I had to jump out of bed every time I heard a noise. After the age of two, she slept very little. I took her to the doctor over and over again. I was told to give her Benadryl at night for a week. It worked, but only while she was on the medication. Once she stopped taking it, she wouldn't sleep.

Jessica was well-known around the neighborhood for her temper tantrums. I would have to fight with her to get her to take a bath. She would scream until I got her into the tub. Once in the water, she would play for hours, then I would have to fight with her to get her out. At age four, she shocked us all. She told us she wanted to jump out the window. She was put in a psychiatric hospital, where I found out she had ADHD (attention deficit disorder). My life was now all about taking care of her. No one wanted to watch her. I got very few breaks from her. Sheena, on the other hand, was a very good child and did not need to be told twice what to do. I didn't realize it, but I was not paying much attention to her. I was too busy fighting with Jessica. Everything—getting her dressed, brushing her teeth, bathing her, putting her to bed—was a battle.

5

Adult Years

One night, Bill and I went to a Halloween party, and Bill got drunk and wrecked the car. When I asked to drive, he hit me. I began to cry, which made him even angrier. He drove very fast, and hit me every time I said something. We got home, and I ran into the bathroom to wipe the blood off my face. I knew he wasn't finished yet, and I knew it was going to be bad. My mom, who had been watching the children, left before I could ask her to stay. As I came out of the bathroom, Bill grabbed me and threw me up against the wall. He started hitting me and yelling at me. He wouldn't stop. As the beating continued, I opened the silverware drawer and pulled out a big knife. "Stop now, or I'll use this," I said.

He grabbed my arm and drew the knife toward his chest. "Do it," he said.

I pulled back and put the knife to my wrist. "I'll do it if you don't stop," I said.

He said, "Let me help you." He grabbed my hand and pulled the knife across my wrist. We both stood there in shock as the blood squirted out. Bill called 911. I fell to the floor. Blood was everywhere. Bill decided not to wait for the ambulance. He wrapped me in a blanket, tied a tourniquet around my wrist, and took me to the hospital. Later, the police came to the hospital and asked me what had happened. I told them I had fallen on a knife. The officer asked me how I had gotten the fat lip and bloody nose. I said it had happened when I fell. I wouldn't tell them what really happened. I was too scared, so I kept it a secret for years to come. I had to have surgery to put my wrist back together.

Bill began working out of town a lot, which was great for me. He was only home for a few days every three weeks. I took care of the kids and worked in my yard, doing landscaping. I was happy. The longer Bill was away, the stronger I became. In 1994, after many attempts, I finally got out of my bad marriage. After one last violent fight, Bill never came after me again.

I went back to school to become a counselor. I had to work with a tutor three times a week to improve my reading and spelling. From 1995 to 1996, I was a domestic-violence counselor and a child advocate. I still had trouble with spelling, so I found a retired grade-school teacher who wasn't afraid to start at kindergarten level. For the first time in my life, I found out what the vowel sounds were. I finally learned the beginning skills of spelling.

I met a guy named Tim, and we became best friends. We would go hunting and fishing together. I could talk to him about anything. I never thought we would be anything more than friends, but when Tim started seeing another girl, I found myself getting jealous. The next thing I knew, it was Tim and I who were dating. We had lots of fun. I called it my "non-reality time." On the weekends, when I didn't have the kids, Tim and I would go on adventures, boating, camping, and mudding out in the woods with the jeep or a four-wheeler. We were close, holding hands all the time. I was falling deeply in love with him. He felt the same. He wanted me to marry him. I loved him dearly, but I did not want to be married. I was still healing from my previous marriage. Later, Tim moved in with me.

This was hard on Jessica. If Tim had a beer, Jessica would get scared and say, "You are going to get drunk like my daddy, and hurt my mommy." If Tim raised his voice, she would run between us and yell, "Stay away from my mommy! Don't hurt her!" I didn't know it at the time, but Jessica had seen the abuse I had endured when I was married to Bill. It traumatized her for many years, and she needed a lot of counseling. A therapeutic staff support (TSS) worker came to my home to help her every day, and a mobile therapist came once a week.

Things were getting stressful at home, but I was on my way to success. I had developed my own prevention-education programs, "Hands Are Not for Hitting" and "What About Self-Esteem?" At first, the programs were just booklets. Then I brought them to life by adding juggling, and later, ventriloquism and puppets. Unfortunately, I had taken on too much, and in 1997, I quit a good-paying job as a domestic-violence counselor to start the SHEP programs. I was doing five programs a day and working on my new program, "Teen Dating Danger." I was also in the middle of filming a children's video called "What About Self-Esteem and Setting Goals?" I was also taking care of my kids and my new live-in boyfriend Tim. I was dealing with Jessica's problem and fighting with school officials, trying to get her more help with her schoolwork. My daughter Sheena was being left out, and I didn't even see it. I was in over my head.

After seven years of dating Tim, I gave in, and we got married. At thirty-one years of age, and six months into our marriage, I was beginning to get depressed. I was embarrassed, and tried to hide it. How could this happen to me? It got worse in time. I started having anxiety attacks. I had trouble doing shows. I couldn't even go to the store.

To help me with the juggling shows, I asked my sixteen-year-old assistant, Peter Morris, to become my full-time partner. I had been working with him since he was ten years old. He was a very good juggler. I began to write him into the show more and more; this helped take the pressure off me. His mom, Judy, and his dad, John, would travel with us and help out when they could. John and Judy never looked down on me because of my illness; they stuck by me through it all. I continued to get worse. I stopped sleeping, and I began to drink to ease my pain. Next, I found myself planning my suicide. No one knew how bad it was, not even me. This was the beginning of a cycle of suicide attempts and hospital visits. I had forgotten everything I had accomplished. I felt like a failure. I felt useless. It took four years to remember where I had come from.

I changed jobs many times; I did landscaping, built decorative ponds, became a carpenter, and did plumbing and electrical work. When I was doing well, I would learn fast, and being taught hands-on made it easy for me to catch on. Later, I began to operate heavy equipment. I loved running the backhoe, and I stuck with it for two years. I learned a lot of skills during those years; I even became a firefighter, which became my new obsession. It also brought me more stress, mainly because I was a woman. I had to work harder to prove myself. Tim didn't like me working for the fire department, and this made more trouble for me. I loved it and didn't see why he couldn't be a part of it with me. He refused.

Adding to the problem, Tim's daughter came to live with us. She could not get along with Jessica. I began to spend a lot of time in bed. I was crying all the time. I stopped taking care of the house. I felt hopeless and sad. My daughter Sheena could not understand what was happening. She got mad at me. At the age of fourteen, she moved out and went to live with my sister. This hurt me deeply. I didn't want her to go, but I was very sick and I couldn't think right. Later, when I was hospitalized for being suicidal, Jessica's father, Bill, found out and took her to live with him. Once again, I was too sick to fight. My life was falling apart. Jessica hated it at her dad's and wanted to come back. This was hard on me.

During this time, I got close to my stepdaughter, Courtney. I felt guilty doing things with her and not my own kids. Tim began to get impatient with me. He developed a bad temper. Our marriage was falling apart. Soon Tim and Courtney were gone, and I was in my big house all by myself, with no job, money, or kids. I was hospitalized fifteen times in four years. I was drinking and making bad choices. I was in self-destruct mode. One morning, after waking up with a bad hangover, I decided to quit drinking. I made up my mind to better my life, whatever it took. I worked on my research on bipolar disorder. I got involved in a University of Pittsburgh study. I took charge of my disorder and my life. I came out of my shell. I was not hiding anymore.

Over the years, I kept notes on my symptoms. From them, I learned what worked for me and what didn't. After reading all my notes, I realized that I had my own get-well plan right in front of me. I was ready to get my life and my kids back. Sheena was getting ready to go to college. Bill had put Jessica in a placement home a year earlier. She was about to get out. I set a goal to get my kids back; I was going to be the mom I had not been for the previous three years. I first asked Sheena to come back, and she did. Then I got Jessica back. I had my kids back, along with another chance to make things right. I was happy. My family said they would help me out as much as they could, and they did. My sister Cindy took Jessica one day a week so I could have a break from her. Sheena helped me with the house and shopping. My dad would get me work now and then running heavy equipment. I spent two or three times a week at the bipolar-research center, being tested and talking to my doctor and my therapist. At night, I read every book I could on bipolar disorder. I took charge of my life and made changes for the better.

6

The Get-Well Plan

The rest of this book is about taking charge of your life and finding ways to cope. I've also included a few more short stories about how I got through the bad times.

Do you feel you have no time to get help? At first, I said I did not have time to go to the doctor or stay in the hospital. Without help, I would push myself to the edge, until I could not even perform my everyday tasks.

If you had cancer or a heart problem, would you go for treatment? How about if you broke your arm? Of course you would. But bipolar disorder is a mental problem. There's stigma attached, so we want to hide it. I spent a lot of time and energy trying to cover up what was happening to me. I always worried that someone would find out. The fact is that if people know about your bipolar disorder, they can help you. I find that if I go for help before it gets too bad, I get back on track sooner. I get to where I'm thinking better and eating and sleeping right, then I go out into the world to try again. The reality is that you can do everything right and still find yourself going into a depressive or manic state. It is how you deal with it that determines the outcome.

Are You Ready?

Accepting that you have bipolar illness is the first step in getting well. The second step is wanting help. Finally, you must be willing to make the changes required to better your life. Most studies reveal a higher rate of treatment success for people with mood disorders when talk therapy is combined with medications and other interventions.

If you have bipolar disorder and an addiction, you need treatment that addresses both conditions. Dealing with only one of these serious problems can delay your recovery.

Signs and Symptoms of Addiction

Drugs
Alcohol
Gambling
Sex

Just as with other diseases, there are many signs and symptoms of addiction. You don't need to experience each and every one to be addicted. The following is a list of symptoms and signs most commonly associated with addiction. Place an *X* next to those that apply to you:

__Using alcohol or other drugs excessively or inappropriately
__Spending a lot of time getting or using chemicals
__Getting high on lower doses of chemicals or needing greater doses to get high
__Having trouble cutting down or stopping once you drink or take drugs
__Experiencing withdrawal symptoms when you do cut down or stop using
__Using alcohol or drugs to avoid or stop withdrawal symptoms
__Using substances even though they are causing problems in your life
__Giving up important activities or losing friendships because of your substance abuse
__Stopping using for a period of time (days, weeks, or months), only to start up again
__Getting into trouble with the law because of alcohol or drug use
__Having blackouts, or forgetting what you did or said while under the influence

Remember, you do not have to show all of these symptoms to have a serious problem with alcohol or drug use. One or two can indicate a serious problem. The more signs you exhibit, the more serious your problem may be. Make a list of other issues you feel could be aggravating your bipolar disorder.

Find a good psychiatrist and therapist and let them know about your issues. Most likely, you will need medications to help you feel better. You need a good psychiatrist to work with you in adjusting your medications as needed. Working with a good doctor can make your treatments more effective, getting you back on the right track. Talk therapy with a good therapist can be a great help in dealing with issues that might aggravate your bipolar disorder. Take your medications and keep your appointments.

Terms to Help You Better Comprehend the World of Psychology

Psychiatrist: A medical doctor who can prescribe medications and is a specialized in the treatment and prevention of mental and emotional disorders.

Psychotherapy or Talk Therapy: Treatment of mental and emotional disorders or related bodily illnesses by examining the person's mind and behavior through conversation.

Psychologist: A professional who specializes in the treatment of mental or emotional disorders.

Psychiatry: A branch of medicine that deals with mental, emotional, or behavioral disorders.

Psychology: The scientific study of mind and behavior.

Getting Organized

Are you ready to get your bipolar life in order? It helps if you get things organized. Prepare yourself for the onset of depression and manic feelings. Talk to your therapist about making a plan of action (what to do and who to call), and have it ready for any problems that arise. Keep things in order in your home and at your job. Pick a special place for all your important papers, like your bills and doctor appointments. This will help you find things when you're not feeling well or thinking straight. Relax! Take time away from all the chaos. Exercise or go for a walk. Take breaks from your ideas. The key to keeping your condition under control is in slowing down and making your life as simple as possible. Don't take on too many projects at once, because when your mind slows down, you may become overwhelmed. This could send you into a depressive phase. Get your sleep. When you are well-rested, you are better able to cope with your problems. I found that when I was drinking, I fell asleep easily, but woke up more often at night. I was not getting a solid night's sleep. I had bad dreams, and I would wake up feeling exhausted, like I hadn't slept at all, so try not to use alcohol to get your-self to sleep. As you feel better and can think more clearly, you will be able to choose how you want to deal with the problems in your life.

A day planner enables you to keep track of all your appointments. This helps keep your stress level down. You can keep important numbers in it, like your crisis numbers and a list of your medications.

Medications and Their Effects

You must understand that from this day forward, medication will most likely be a part of your daily life. It is important to learn all you can about what you are taking and how each medication makes you feel. This will help you in understanding what works for you, enabling you to more clearly explain to your doctor how the medication is working. This allows him or her to adjust your dosage accordingly. Each medication will affect you differently. When you get depressed or manic, you may stop eating right, and then the medication can affect you in different ways. When you're manic, you may need more medication to help you sleep at night. This can help to slow down the racing thoughts in your head that will not let you get a good night's rest.

When you get depressed, you may need more medication to help lift you from your feelings. Lithium is naturally occurring salt. It is the drug of choice for mania. Other medications, however, have been used when lithium is ineffective or when a person is unable to take it. It is very important to have blood work done when you take lithium. Checking your blood levels every one to three months will assure that your lithium level is where it needs to be. I cannot stress enough how important it is to eat right and drink plenty of water when you are on medications.

Toxic Lithium Levels

When food and fluid intake is less than recommended, the lithium level in your bloodstream can become higher and cause a clammy feeling, shakiness, tremulousness, nausea, and constipation. When you drink excessive amounts of alcohol or caffeine, it can dehydrate you and cause your lithium level to become toxic. Be sure to tell your doctor if you drink alcohol or take street drugs or over-the-counter medications, because this can affect the way your medication works. Your doctor may make unnecessary changes, which could cause a delay in finding the right medicine for you. Work closely with your doctor to assure that the amount of medication you are taking is right for you. This takes time, but is well worth it. Make a list of the medications and dosages you take and keep the list with you. A good place for this list is in your day planner. That way you can keep all of your information in one place.

Making your Medication Chart

This is an example of how to create and fill out your personalized medication checklist:

This is just an example. You should add or delete options based on your needs.

It is important to keep track of all the medications you are taking. This helps to track if there are any reactions between them. Also note if you have a mood change while taking that medication.

When making your chart, be sure to make extra blank spaces for use if you get prescribed new medications or other variables come into play, such as cold medication, pain pills, antibiotics, etc., so you can write them in as well. Also be sure to note any as needed, or "rescue medications" that you may be prescribed. Their use is also important to note, their frequency and duration.

First make your chart. I like to use the first column to list my medications. I also like to use one column for each day, using the same chart for an entire week. You can certainly use a daily chart or a monthly chart, but for me, the weekly method seems to work best.

Next, write the date at the top of the chart.

Then fill in the weight you are for the first day of the week.

At the top of the chart write in next to the day of the week the date for each day...

Use the first column of the chart for what medications you are taking, how many milligrams that you take daily, and the time you take it.

Now it is time to keep track of your medications. Be honest. If you miss a dose, leave it blank. If you take more or less, write that in also. Consistency is important. Without detailed and accurate information, you will not be able to accurately track symptoms, hindering your results.

Date 1/2/2006 Weight 149			Mon 2		Tues		Wed		Thurs		Fri		Sat		Sun	
Medication	mg	Time	Time	Mg	Time	mg	Time	mg	Time	mg	Time	mg	Time	mg	Time	mg
Lithobid	675	9 Pm	9 pm	675	10 PM	675										
Seroquel	400	9 Pm	9 pm	400	10pm	200										
Other																
Lithobid	300	7am	7am	300												
Pain pill																
Seroquel	25	7am	7am	25												
Vitamin		7am	7am													

Be sure to keep a list of side effects you may be experiencing and share them with your doctor as soon as possible.

Medication Box

A seven-day pillbox is one of the best ways to keep your medications in order. A pillbox helps you keep track of what and how much medicine you should take, and when. This also will help keep your stress level down. It also helps to keep notes on how the medications make you feel. Document any side effects you are experiencing and let your doctor know. If the bad side effects outweigh the good, you may need to talk to your doctor about a change in your medications.

Some Side Effects of Medications:

Decrease or increase of appetite
Drowsiness
Headaches and body aches
Dry mouth
Sleeplessness
Sexual side effects
Nausea
Constipation
Diarrhea
Agitation
Shakiness
Rash
Acne
Hand tremor

Since I am not qualified to discuss medications, I asked Dr. Turkin to write some information on medication for my book:

Medication is an integral part of treatment for this disorder. This is a big topic, and I refer the reader for greater detail to advocacy groups, such as the Depression and Bipolar Support Alliance (DBSA); professional ones, such as the American Psychiatric Association (APA); or government institutions, such as the National Institute of Mental Health (NIMH). Since there has been such an explosion in research and knowledge in this field, ideally medication management of this condition should be under the supervision of a qualified psychiatrist.

Mood stabilizers are the mainstays of treatment for bipolar disorder. These are medications that make further episodes less frequent and/or severe, as well as treating acute episodes of any polarity. While no medication currently available completely fulfills that ideal, most experts would agree that several medications from a family called Anticonvulsants, others called Atypical Antipsychotics, and Lithium are mood stabilizers, and they should form the foundation of pharmacological treatment for this disorder.

Anticonvulsants are so-named because they have anti-seizure properties. Those with the most proven value in bipolar disorder are Valproate (Depakote and others), Lamictal (Lamotrigine), and Carbamazepine (Tegretol, Equetro). They are not interchangeable, and some people respond better to one than another. Valproate and Carbamazepine are felt to be more effective for manic or mixed states, and Lamictal for depressive ones. It is important to have periodic blood tests to monitor the level of Valproate and Carbamazepine in one's body, as well as to detect the rare occurrence of effects on the liver or other organs. There are many other anticonvulsants that have been studied to some degree in this illness (Topamax, Neurontin, Gabatril, Keppra, Zonisamide), but their place in bipolar therapy has not been proven.

Atypical Antipsychotics received their name from the fact that they are different in effect from the older "typical" medications and that they were first developed for psychoses, such as schizophrenia. They are all proven anti-manic as well as preventative in postponing further manic episodes. There is some data for most of them that they may have benefit in acute as well as maintenance treatment for the depressed side as well. This is an area of active research. They include Risperidone (Risperdal), Olanzapine (Zyprexa), Quetiapine (Seroquel), Aripiprazole (Abilify) and Ziprasidone (Geodon). Clozaril (Clozapine) and others are also in this group and effective, but they aren't used first-line due to unusual but potentially serious side effects. These drugs are roughly equally effective, but vary principally in their side-effect profiles.

Lithium is still considered the gold-standard mood stabilizer. It has been used for more than fifty years. Anyone with bipolar disorder who hasn't been sufficiently stable deserves a trial of this medication. It is very important that blood tests for the level of the drug and other parameters are monitored regularly and that all providers of medication be aware of your entire medication list, to avoid interactions with Lithium.

Antidepressants are very useful for unipolar depression, anxiety, and other disorders, but their place in the treatment of bipolar disorder is still being studied and debated amongst the experts in this field. All agree that they shouldn't be used alone in this disorder, to avoid switches into mania or hypomania or acceleration of cycles.

The FDA (Food and Drug Administration) approved the combination of Olanzapine and fluoxetine for bipolar depression, and it is likely that others will also be approved for this indication in the near future.

Other Treatment Options

Electroconvulsive therapy (ECT), sometimes referred to as electroshock therapy, is an effective biologic intervention for major depression, the disorder for which it is most frequently administered. ECT remains a subject of much controversy. I was totally against the procedure until I saw what it did for my father.

Dad found out at age sixty that he had bipolar disorder. Up until then, he had been a very creative person. He had built the number-one furnace company in the world. He was a self-made millionaire and had everything he could ever want in life. Then he fell into a deep depression. I watched as he went downhill. He was no longer thinking right, and he sold his business without even telling me. Then he announced that he was going to sell the dream home he had built in the country. I told him he would regret it, but he wouldn't listen. He decided to build a new home in town, but his condition was worsening. He couldn't remember what he was doing. The contractors were getting frustrated, because Dad would hire two workers for the same job. His wife, Kim, asked me to come over and help them finish the project. I agreed, and did as much as I could.

Dad got so bad that he would shuffle his feet as he walked. He functioned at a very slow pace. He had no expression left on his face, and he could not remember what he did from one minute to the next. Kim and I talked and decided to put him in the hospital. He went, then came home, but he still was not doing well. It was like he had Alzheimer's or Parkinson's disease. I sent him to doctor after doctor.

Finally, Dr. Turkin agreed to take my dad as a patient. He tried to help my father for almost a year, but Dad was not consistent with his medications. He also missed many of his appointments. He did not see any positive results. Dr. Turkin felt he could not help him anymore. He recommended shock therapy. I didn't like the idea, but we were at the end of the road. There was nothing else we could do for him. My dad went to Neuropsychiatric Associates, Inc. for an interview with Dr. Steven B. Gelfand, MD. The doctor felt my dad needed treatment, and decided to admit him to the hospital. Dad had three shock treatments in the first week. He was released, but he had to go back once a week for nine weeks for fol-low-up ECT treatments. He got better. After a year, I got my dad back. He was normal again. This was a miracle. I could not believe the difference in him. When medication and talk therapy didn't work, ECT came through. Still, I would only use this as a last resort, when all else fails.

7

Monitoring Your Symptoms

I have a symptom checklist that I've developed over the past five years. I use my list every day. It allows me to be honest with myself about how I am doing. It also lets me know when I need to seek help before things spin out of control. I have three sections to check each day: morning, afternoon, and evening. This helps me to recognize if I am "cycling" (fluctuating between manic and depressed states with periods of normality) throughout the week, or even cycling throughout the day. There was a time when I was so bad that I needed an hourly chart. I would have to check my symptoms chart every hour. As I got better, I would resume using the daily checklist.

I made up my chart on the computer. If you don't have access to a computer, you can just draw one on a piece of paper and make copies. I keep all my charts in a binder, including my medication chart. When I visit my doctor, I share this information with him.

This is my weekly chart I put together over the past five years. This is how I kept track of my symptoms. It is what helped me to see what changes I needed to make and helped me to understand my illness. The charts let me know when it was time to go for more help. I also used this to help me better communicate with my doctor and therapist.

Making a Symptom Chart Checklist

Example of order of symptom checklist chart.
This is an example of how to put your chart all together.
Under each symptom heading, add as many lines as needed to add your new symptoms.

Date _____ Weight _____	Monday			Tuesday			Wednesday			Thursday			Friday			Saturday			Sunday		
	AM	N	PM	AM	N	PM	AM	N	PM	AM	N	PM	AM	N		AM	N	PM	AM	N	PM
If applicable Menstrual cycle																					
Stressor of the day																					
Notes																					
Manic																					
Depressed																					
Suicidal																					
Sleep habits																					
Eating habits																					
Abdominal problems																					
Substance use																					
Sex drive																					

How to Put Your Symptom Chart All Together

How to put your chart together

This is a sample symptom checklist chart for you to use to start your own.
Write the date in, then write the dates over the days of the week.
Fill in your weight for the first day of the week.

Date _____ Weight	8th Monday	9th Tuesday	10th Wednesday	11th Thursday	12th Friday	13th Saturday	14th Sunday
As for women: Your menstrual cycle may play a part in your mood swings and you may fall into depression easily. It is something to watch for so as you could be prepared for it.							
Do you have your menstrual cycle							

Notes:

Sometimes I write notes on my chart to let me know more of what is going on at that time.
This helps me know why I may have felt the way I did at that time, for exempla was it from a stressor in my life that made me feel like I did.

Notes							
Stressor of the day							

When you make your own chart you can fill in the symptoms that you feel you are having.
Then you can see if it is a symptom of bipolar or if it is a stressor of yours
For the first few months you may need to add symptoms as they occur, so be sure to leave some blank spaces to add your new symptoms.
For the symptom checklist chart, I use the following system:
I put an XX after the question if I feel strongly about how I feel.
If I am feeling somewhat bad or good, I just use an X.
If I do not feel all that bad or good, I put a / or leave it blank.
Put your x in the box of the time of day your symptom occurs AM, N or PM

Manic	Am	N	Pm

Date ____ Weight ____	8th Monday			9th Tuesday			10th Wednesday			11th Thursday			12th Friday			13th Saturday			14th Sunday		
	Am	N	Pm	Am	N	Pm	Am	N	Pm	Am	N	Pm	Am	N	Pm	Am	N	Pm	Am	N	Pm
Do you feel Manic					X	X															
Racing thoughts						X	XX														
Elated mood					X		X														
Rapid speech						X															
Bursts of energy					X	X	X														
Less need for sleep						X															
Irritability							X														

Date _____
Weight _____

	Monday			Tuesday			Wednesday			Thursday			Friday			Saturday			Sunday		
Depressed	Am	N	Pm	Am	N	Pm	Am	N	Pm	Am	N	Pm	Am	N	Pm	Am	N	Pm	Am	N	Pm
Do you feel Depressed		X	XX																		
Memory loss																					
Negative		X	XX																		
Paranoid		X	X																		
Anxiety		X	XX																		
Cry a lot		X	XX																		
Very jumpy																					
Sensitive to noise																					
Feel like you want to run away																					
Cannot feel happy			XX																		
Lack of motivation		X	X																		
Stay in bed																					
Want to do self harm			X																		
Did you hurt yourself																					

Date / Weight	8th Monday			9th Tuesday			10th Wednesday			11th Thursday			12th Friday			13th Saturday			14th Sunday		
	Am	N	Pm	Am	N	Pm	Am	N	Pm	Am	N	Pm	Am	N	Pm	Am	N	Pm	Am	N	Pm
Suicidal		X	XX																		
Do not care about anything		X	XX																		
Thinking about dying		X	XX																		
Want to die		X	XX																		
Making plans to kill yourself			X																		
Have the things to kill yourself			X																		

CALL FOR HELP NOW IF YOU FELT THIS WAY!

Your sleep habits play a large part in helping to show if you are depressed or manic.
*Write the time in the **Pm** or **Am** box what time you went to bed.*
*Then write in the **Am** or **Pm** box what time you woke up.*
Next write in the hours of sleep you got that night.
Then mark an X if you took a nap or stayed in bed all day.

Date _____ Weight _____	Monday			Tuesday			Wednesday			Thursday			Friday			Saturday			Sunday		
Sleep habits	Am	N	Pm	Am	N	Pm	Am	N	Pm	Am	N	Pm	Am	N	Pm	Am	N	Pm
Time went to sleep																		
Time woke up																		
Hours slept																		
Hard to fall asleep			X															
Woke up often			X															
Sleep all day																		
Did you take a nap		X																
Laid in bed awake		X																

Appetite increase or decrease and /or abdominal problems may be related to your medication, Bipolar illness or a stressor in your life.

Date ____ Weight ____	Monday			Tuesday			Wednesday			Thursday			Friday			Saturday			Sunday		
	AM	N	PM	AM	N	PM	AM	N	PM	AM	N	PM	AM	N	PM	AM	N	PM	AM	N	PM
Eating habits																					
Decrease of appetite		X	X																		
Loss of appetite			XX																		
Increase of appetite																					
Forget to eat																					
Abdominal problems																					
Nausea			X																		
Vomiting																					
Diarrhea																					
Constipation			X																		

Substance use: This will help you see how caffeine, alcohol or drugs use can affect your bipolar illness.

Write the number of caffeine or alcohol drinks you had that day.

If you have any other addictions you may make a chart for them as well.

Substance use	Monday			Tuesday			Wednesday			Thursday			Friday			Saturday			Sunday		
	Am	N	Pm	Am	N	Pm	Am	N	Pm	Am	N	Pm	Am	N	Pm	Am	N	Pm	Am	N	Pm
Caffeine drinks	2	2	1																		
alcohol Number of drinks			6																		
feel like you needed to be drunk or high			X																		
Feel like you need to stop the pain			XX																		
Did you get drunk or high			X																		
How many cigarettes did you smoke	2	6	9																		
Did you smoke more			X																		

Sex drive
This is just for you to keep tract of your own actions
The sex drive part is to help you to see if you are being promiscuous.
This is something people with bipolar illness need to watch out for.
If you know what is going on you can try to prevent it and possible save your relationship with your significant other.
Plus prevent an unwanted pregnancy or contracting STD.

Date ___ Weight ___	Monday			Tuesday			Wednesday			Thursday			Friday			Saturday			Sunday		
Sex drive	Am	N	Pm	Am	N	Pm	Am	N	Pm	Am	N	Pm	Am	N	Pm	Am	N	Pm	Am	N	Pm
Increased sex drive		X	X	X	X	X															
Decreases sex drive						X															
Promiscuity			X																		
Flirtatious		X	X																		
Did you have sex			X																		
With whom			X																		

Christine's Symptom Chart Checklist

Christine's symptom checklist chart

This is an example of one of the charts I completed while monitoring my symptoms. As you look at my weekly symptom chart, you can see that I went from manic to depressed to suicidal in a week's time. This is a true copy of my weekly symptom chart from March 2003. Back in March, after looking at my chart and seeing how bad I truly was feeling, I called my doctor and admitted myself to the adult behavioral health unit. I stayed until the suicidal thoughts passed. Remember, it is better to be safe than sorry. Get help when you need it.

Weight 138 / Date 2003	10 Monday			11 Tuesday			12 Wednesday			13 Thursday			14 Friday			15 Saturday			16 Sunday		
Menstrual cycle	yes			yes																	
Stressor	Money												Money			Kids/house					
Notes				Juggling shows												Bad day			Bad day		
	Am	N	Pm	Am	N	Pm	Am	N	Pm	Am	N	Pm	Am	N	Pm	Am	N	Pm	Am	N	Pm
Manic																					
Are you manic?	X	x	x	x	x	x	x	xx	x	x						x	x				
Racing thoughts	x	x	x	x	x	x	x	xx	x	x						x	x				
Hyperactive	x	x	x	x	x	x	x	xx	xx												
Elated mood	x		x	x		x	x	x	xx												
Rapid speech							x	x													
Bursts of energy	x	x	x	x	x	x	x	x	x												
Need less sleep	x	x	x	x	x	x	x	x	x												

Weight 138 Date 2003	10 Monday	11 Tuesday	12 Wednesday	13 Thursday	14 Friday	15 Saturday	16 Sunday
Depressed					x x	x x x	xx xx xx
Do you feel depressed?					x x	x x x	xx xx x
Difficulty concentrating							
Irritability						x x	xx x x
Forget full						x x	xx x x
Memory loss						x x	xx x x
Paranoid						x x	xx x x
Cry a lot					x x	x x	xx x x
Anxiety						x x	xx x x
Very jumpy						x x	xx x x
Sensitive to noise						x x	x x x
Feel like you want to run away						x	x x x
Cant feel happy							
Want to cut						x	x x x
Want to hurt yourself							xx xx xx
Did you harm yourself?							x x x
Feel negative							x xx

Suicidal																x			x	xx
Do not care about anything																			x	xx
Thinking about dying																			x	xx
Want to die																			x	xx
Making plans to kill yourself																			x	xx
Have the stuff to kill your self																			x	x
Eating habits	x	x	x	x	x		x	x	x										x	x
Loss of appetite	x	x	x	x	x	x	x	x	x					x					x	x
Forget to eat	x	x	x	x	x	x	x	x	x									x		
Abdominal pain																				
Nausea							x													
Vomiting				x			x													
Diarrhea																				
Constipation	x				x				x			x								
Substance use																				
Caffeine drink	3	4	2	1	2	3	2	2	1	3	2	2	3	2	3	4	3	2		
k																				
How much alcohol?	4		5		7	1			2		6			9	6	9				
Did you feel like you needed to be drunk or high?							x			x		xx		xx	xx	xx				
Feel like you needed to stop the pain																				
Did you get drunk or high?						x				x		x		x	xx	xx				
How many cigarettes did you smoke?	5	4	4	4	3	4	5	5	5	9	8	9	10	9	10	11	10	11		
Did you smoke more?										x	x	x				x	x	x		

Date 2003 Weight 138	Monday			Tuesday			Wednesday			Thursday			Friday			Saturday			Sunday		
	Am	N	Pm	Am	N	Pm	Am	N	Pm	Am	N	Pm	Am	N	Pm	Am	N	Pm	Am	N	Pm
Sex Drive																					
Increased sex drive	/	/	/	/	/	/					X		X		X	X			X	X	X
Decreased sex drive							X	X	X												
Promiscuity												X			X			X			X
Flirtatious												X			X			X			X
Did you have sex												X									
With whom												?									?
Sleep habits																					
Time went to sleep	12			2			7		11	2		11	7		10	7		11	10		11
Time woke up	5			5			7			5			7			7			10		
Hours slept	5			3			8			3			9			8			12		
Took a nap																					
Laid in bed awake			x			x			x			x							x		
Hard to fall asleep									x			x									
Woke up often									x			x								x	
Dreams feel real									x			x									x

Simple Symptom Chart Checklist

Simple symptom chart
You may use this chart when you are feeling better and have a better grasp of your symptom.

	Monday			Tuesday			Wednesday			Thursday			Friday			Saturday			Sunday		
Date _____ Weight _____																						
Menstrual cycle																						
Stressor of the day																						
Notes																						
	AM	N	PM	AM	N	PM	AM	N	PM	AM	N	PM	AM	N	PM	AM	N	PM	AM	N	PM
Manic																						
Stable																						
Mild																						
Moderate																						
Severe																						
Depressed																						
Stable																						
Mild																						
Moderate																						
Severe																						
Suicidal																						
Stable																						
Mild																						
Moderate																						
Severe																						
Stressed out																						
Stable																						
Mild																						
Moderate																						
Severe																						

8

Signs and Symptoms of Mania Test

Manic Test

Take this test and then take it with you to your doctor and let him or her see it. Like other illnesses, bipolar disorder has certain signs and symptoms. Their exact patterns and severity vary among individuals. You don't have to experience all of them to have a diagnosis of bipolar disorder.

Place an *X* next to the changes you have experienced:

__I feel high. I am exceptionally cheerful, enthusiastic, and optimistic.
__I feel that my ideas come and go unusually easily, as if my thoughts are racing.
__I feel an urge to communicate by phone or letters.
__I feel a strong desire to reconnect with people I haven't seen or talked with in a long time.
__I have increased self-confidence or an exaggerated sense of my own abilities.
__I have boundless energy.
__I am very busy and start many projects.
__I have so many thoughts and ideas all at once that I find it difficult to express them.
__I am too busy to sleep and I rarely feel tired.
__I feel warm, extroverted, and sociable. I'm very comfortable introducing myself to others and making new friends.
__I spend a lot of time on social, political, or religious causes.

__I become very talkative; I may not let others get a word in.

__I don't listen to anyone else.

__I say whatever comes to mind.

__I experience a flood of thoughts that don't always seem connected.

__My conversation jumps from topic to topic. My ideas become jumbled.

__I have difficulty staying focused on tasks and completing projects.

__I take on many projects, jumping from one activity to another.

__I feel much livelier than usual and I'm full of energy.

__I am constantly active and have the pleasant sensation of never being tired.

__My energy is so high that it exhausts or irritates others.

__I have high sexual energy.

__I am very flirtatious.

__I engage in inappropriate or dangerous sexual activity.

__I frequently change jobs, place of residence, friends, and hobbies.

__I feel impulsive and make poor decisions.

__I spend a lot of money or make poor financial decisions.

__I have frequent and serious conflicts with other people.

Symptom Page

Signs and Symptoms of Bipolar Disorder

Symptoms of Mania:

High self-esteem

Inability to sleep

Loss of appetite

Boundless energy

Racing thoughts

Doing many projects at one time

Obsessing over whatever it is you are doing, to the exclusion of all else

Exhibiting psychotic features

Inability to gauge time

Claim to be God, Superman, or Satan

Claim to have superpowers

Hypomania

Hypomania is a milder form of mania lasting at least four days. The individual's mood is elevated, expansive, or irritable, with signs of mania. Symptoms, however, are less severe and may not impair social or occupational functioning. Psychotic features are absent.

Mixed Manic Depressed Symptoms

Thoughts racing even faster
Too much information coming in at one time
Trying to do too much at once
Becoming irritable
Becoming very forgetful
Lying in bed at night with many thoughts running through your head
Inability to sleep
Waking up often through the night
When sleeping, your dreams seem real
Experiencing nightmares
Eating poorly; loss of appetite
Getting stressed out easily
Wringing your hands
Feeling edgy and jumpy
Becoming sensitive to noise
Smoking more than usual
Becoming very tired, but still unable to sleep
Having anxiety attacks
Heart pounding or racing
Feeling overwhelmed by everyday tasks
Crying a lot
Having a lot of negative thoughts
Feeling sad and depressed
Experiencing headaches
Feeling sick and having body aches

Thoughts of giving up come to mind
Inability to feel happiness
Feeling the desire to drink or take drugs
Finding yourself behaving more flirtatiously
Becoming more sexually active
Feeling the urge to hurt yourself
Following through on that urge
Becoming paranoid
Stopping caring
Wishing you were dead
Entertaining thoughts of suicide

Symptoms of Depression

A feeling of slowing down
Unhappiness
Loss of energy
Inability to find enjoyment in life
Increase or decrease in appetite
Restlessness
Increased crying
Lack of concentration
Difficulty in making everyday decisions
Difficulty in performing the smallest task
Very negative thinking
Self-neglect (poor hygiene, etc.)
Become withdrawn and isolated
Feelings of worthlessness

Suicidal Symptoms

Feeling that you need to stop the pain you are having.
Feeling that life is not worth living
Having thoughts of dying
Loss of hope for the future

Writing a will or good—by note.

Have a specific plan of how you would end your life.

Spend most of your energy and time planning and thinking about how you would kill yourself.

Suicide and Depression

When the depression sets in and you're feeling hopeless, it's hard to see the light at the end of the tunnel. The pain you feel is real, and yes, it hurts. Sometimes you cannot even get out of bed. It becomes hard to make even simple decisions. But it will pass, and it will get better with time and help from your doctor or therapist and medication.

Suicide

When I get suicidal, the plan pops right into my head. I have three different plans that are well-thought-out from my past experiences. This makes it very dangerous for me. I have to get help right away. I call my counselor or doctor and set an appointment, or talk to him on the phone. Sometimes that alone helps. I tell myself that if I can get adequate sleep, I'll overcome this. If I don't drink, it's less likely I will cut or hurt myself or make bad choices. If I feel like I'm spinning out of control, I go to the hospital for a few days. Knowing what to do and making the right choices is what makes all the difference.

Suicide Prevention Plan

The feelings of suicide have passed, and you're feeling better. This is your chance to make a suicide-prevention plan. The first thing you must do is to get rid of your weapon or weapons of choice. Throw that stash of pills away. Give your guns to someone for safekeeping, or better yet, sell them. Rip up any good-bye notes you have. Keep close at hand a list of phone numbers of people to whom you can turn in times of crisis. This will make it more difficult to follow through on your suicidal feelings. You will have bought some extra time, and that may give your deadly thoughts a chance to subside. Write yourself a note. Tell yourself how good you feel now. Congratulate yourself for not following through on your plan. Express your joy in being alive. Save the note. The next time you find yourself in a vulnerable state, read it and understand that the feelings will pass and things will be okay.

Suicide: The Forever Decision, by Paul G. Quinnett, is the best book I have ever read on suicide. It was a major help to me. It allowed me to see the reality of what could happen if I attempted suicide.

Have a Plan of Action

Make a list of important phone numbers:
Hotline/Hospital
Therapist/Psychiatrist
Family
Friends

Keep your phone list with you at all times Make a list of the things you can do to feel better; for instance, getting more sleep. Keep this information in your day planner and keep updating the symptom checklist.

Hospitalization

You may require hospitalization to adjust your medication, or if you feel you may hurt yourself. It's okay to ask for help. There is absolutely nothing wrong with going into a hospital and getting treatment.

9

Falling into Depression

To be perfectly honest with you, I was in a mixed state of manic depression when I wrote this portion of the book. As my mixed manic-depressive state continued, I found myself forgetting things. People were getting mad at me. I kept a close eye on my symptoms chart. I was getting worse. I called my doctor, and he agreed to see me right away. He changed my medication. From that point, I took on one problem at a time, dealt with it, and moved to the next one. I reminded myself of my accomplishments and used positive thinking. This helped in speeding up my recovery. As I felt myself getting more depressed, I started thinking that I couldn't do this anymore. I couldn't get anything done. I couldn't think right. I had all these ideas at once, and I wanted to do them all. I would start one thing and then walk into the other room and start something else. In less than an hour, I would find myself working on four new projects.

Once, I was doing the dishes. I went to my office to get something and started writing notes for this book. The next thing I knew, I was working on a room I had been remodeling. I started putting down the new floor. I went to the garage to get more nails, but saw some wood that I thought I could use for trim. I started doing that, but was soon back working on the book.

This is very difficult to deal with. It's so hard when everything seems out of your control. I tell myself that it won't always be like this, and that keeps me going. I will have good times again. It's hard to see that when you're not doing well. You start wondering: *Why me?*

My manic episode was followed by a period of deep depression. I knew I could fall back into negative thinking. This was a very difficult time for me. My mind slowed down to a crawl. My ideas were gone; I couldn't even make a simple decision. I could feel myself wanting to go back to my old habits. I was thinking negatively, I didn't want to eat, and I felt the urge to start drinking again, so I called my therapist, Mark Stoltz. Talk therapy makes a difference; Mark is my main support system. I am very lucky to have him. He is the best therapist I have ever worked with.

As I got worse, the stress increased. My mind was lost in an echo. I couldn't remember things. I would make a list of things to do and lose it. It was hard to do simple, everyday tasks. I would find myself crying for no reason. I wanted to drink, but chose not to. My mind was in hell. My temper flared. I was frustrated and very irritable, I felt as if I were falling apart. I didn't think I could take anymore. By the end of the week, I was so down and depressed that I became suicidal. It's very hard to think right when feeling this way, so I called my friend Robby, who reminded me that I had some juggling shows the next weekend. It was important to me to make it to my shows. We talked until two in the morning. It helped calm me down, and I managed to talk myself out of suicide. I went to bed and got some sleep. Monday came around, and I was still not doing well. I talked with my therapist on the phone. Just knowing he was there was help for me. I went to my doctor the next day. He adjusted my medication again. I spoke some more with my therapist and saw the doctor again.

Another type of helpful therapy is called enhanced clinical intervention (ECI). The bipolar study is trying this as a part of their research. In my experience, this type of intense talk therapy gets you back on the right track faster. It gives you the hope you need to keep going. When you have bipolar disorder, you need medication, but you also need talk therapy. With help and all of this intervention, I came out of my depression in a week's time.

The Manic Times

It is important to learn how to control yourself when you become manic. It can be hard with so many ideas flooding in. You want to get on with things. You charge through your work, getting it done at any cost. Slow down! Yes, it feels good to accomplish things, but not to the exclusion of all else. Is it really worth it when the end result is crashing, or even losing a friend or spouse? Give yourself a break. Take time to do other things. When you are in a manic phase, you must learn to try to control it. If you're feeling this way and can recognize the symptoms, call your doctor. Perhaps your medications need to be adjusted.

Mania Can Lead to Mixed Mania and Depression

I was manic for fifteen years. It was who I was. The stress kept building up, and all the little problems began to get to me. I went into a mixed manic-depressive state. I began to crash. I had so much going on that I couldn't keep up with it all. This came at a time in my life when I was going places. I had a new program out on self-esteem. I had a new video out, and assembly programs booked in many schools. My dreams were coming true, but I wasn't taking time to stop and smell the roses. I did not make time for my family or my friends. I worked on my programs day and night, sleeping very little.

My relationship with my husband, Tim, was falling apart. He was getting upset with me. He wanted me to spend more time with him. I knew I was losing the man I loved, but I thought it was entirely his fault. *How dare he try to hold me back from my job and my dreams?* I failed to see that he needed some of my time too.

I thought everyone was trying to hold me back. All I could think about was getting my programs done. My problems were getting bigger, and I was beginning to feel depressed. I found I could not get all I wanted done, like I could before. I was slowing down, and I had way too much on my plate. I felt overwhelmed. I tried to keep up. I pushed myself, not knowing I needed help. I tried desperately to keep going. This made me feel even worse. I didn't know what was happening to me.

Pain and sadness set in. I fell back into my old ways of thinking. To help ease the pain, I started drinking again; soon I was drinking every night. Things got worse. I couldn't see any way out. I started thinking about dying. Before I knew it, I was planning my death. I pushed everyone away. I stopped talking to my friends. I got into fights with Tim for no reason. I was tired, but could not sleep. I couldn't eat. I felt sick all the time and cried a lot. I wasn't keeping up with my housework, and I got even more stressed when things were out of place. I had no idea how bad I really was. I could not see a way out. I began planning my suicide. I got myself a gun and wrote a suicide note.

My plan was to get all of my business in order and go to the woods and shoot myself. I was planning to do it in two weeks, but after a few days, I felt I just could not take it anymore. I just wanted some relief. I wasn't seeing any light at the end of the tunnel. I got my gun, grabbed some beer, and took a back road deep into the woods. I began to drink, so I would have the guts to pull the trigger. I didn't want some kid to find my body with my head blown off, so I called the police on my cell phone and let them know where they could find my body. Maybe it was a call for help; I do not know. I do know that it really felt like I was going to do it. The police called me and tried to talk to me. I told them to leave me alone. I hung up the phone and took the safety off my nine-millimeter. I put the gun to my head. Then, all of a sudden, a four-wheel drive came up the path. I quickly put the gun down.

It was a couple going for a ride. They came up toward me, turned around, and went back down the path. When they got to the main road, they were pulled over by a state policeman, who thought it might be me. The policeman got a four-wheel drive and came in after me. I was sitting in my Blazer, crying, with the gun to my head, when I spotted the vehicle coming up the path. I jumped out, yelling. I wanted him to go away. He had found me too soon, and I was angry. I sought protection behind a big tree, as did the policeman. I explained that I only wanted to hurt myself, not him. I asked him to go away. I didn't want him to see me blow my head off. He ordered me to put the gun down. I refused. I said, "You will hurt me if I put it down."

"I will not," he said. "I will just come over there and give you a big hug." I had the safety off and the gun to my head. More police came up the path, and I told them to stay back. I was crying. An officer brought up the subject of my daughters, Jessica and Sheena. He kept repeating their names. I got mad at first. I told him to shut up. In the end, I gave up the gun. It took them three hours to talk me out of it. I put the gun on the ground. One cop jumped on it. The first cop kept his promise and gave me a big hug. I was taken to a hospital, and I stayed there for about four weeks. I got the help I needed and I was feeling better, but when I went home, I quickly went manic. It wasn't long before I was in way over my head, all over again.

For four years, I went through these cycles of intense highs and deep, dark lows. I would seek out help, get back on my feet, feel better, and then do it again. A time came when I just stopped doing all the things I loved to do. I stopped the programs. I stopped juggling. I became a housewife who didn't do much else but care for the kids and clean the house. I felt so useless. I didn't dare attempt my programs, for fear I'd get sick again. I got so depressed that I stopped paying the bills. I was neglecting the house and the kids. Everything over-whelmed me. I drank every time a crisis arose. It took me four years to see that I needed to do the things I loved, but I needed moderation. I had to change the way I did things and stop drinking. Whenever I quit the booze, things started coming around. It's not easy to stop, but as time passes, it becomes easier. I learned that I needed to change the way I thought and lived my life. I made up my mind to get better, and that was half the battle.

Take time to enjoy your life. You have the extreme good fortune to be here right now, so do the things that you like to do. The more you see your life as the immense opportunity that it is, the more richness you will uncover. There is a path that leads to the best in life, and the starting point is where you are right now. Pause for a moment and consider your many blessings. Make the effort, and work your way into the light of achievement.

Survival

You may think you want to die—until you have to fight for your life. I went to my camp on the eve of hunting season. I was feeling depressed and suicidal. I just wanted to be alone. I had my .30-30 rifle with me, and I was thinking about ending it all. I drank a few beers, lay down with my gun by my side, and decided to go to sleep and see how I felt in the morning. I dozed off.

Suddenly I was awakened by a crackling noise. I opened my eyes and saw flames shooting out of the wall. Black smoke billowed all around me. It was so thick, it choked me. I felt beside me and grabbed the fire extinguisher. I rolled onto the floor and aimed the extinguisher at the drawer, where the orange flames were coming from. I pulled the pin and squeezed the trigger. A slight spray dribbled out of it. It was malfunctioning. I knew I had to get out fast. I reached to get my cell phone. I grabbed it "then," tried to find my way out. I could feel my fingers burning as I felt my way out of the camp. I was desperate to get out and stay alive. I found the door. When I opened it, the air rushed in and the camp exploded into flames. I rolled out onto the ground and looked up as the flames climbed to the top of the trees. I crawled about fifteen feet away. There was an explosion. The propane tank blew up like a bomb. The place where I had just been sleeping was engulfed in flames.

I lay on the ground, watching my life flash before my eyes. Pieces of the campsite were falling all around me. I called 911, and then everything went blank. When I came to, the fire chief was standing over me. At the time, I thought I was fine, and told him so. The next thing I remembered, I was in an ambulance, with a tube running down my throat. Someone was yelling, "Stay with us! Come on, you can do it!" Then I heard someone else say I was crashing. I lost consciousness. I was suffering from smoke inhalation. I woke up in the hospital, feeling very weak, but happy to be alive. I had gone to bed that night thinking of ending my life, and I woke up fighting to live. I had my chance to die, and I chose to live.

From that day forward, I knew I really wanted to live. I just had to let the bad thoughts pass, and I would be fine. My life may be full of chaos, but I have a more positive outlook on life. I choose to think good thoughts. This influences how I perceive whatever comes my way, and my thoughts determine how I react, so I try to keep a positive attitude in every situation. I choose to take the path that will lead me in the right direction. I try to find the good in whatever comes my way.

Take the better approach to your problems. Choose the positive alternative and set about putting it into practice. Bipolar disorder is a roller coaster of ups and downs. Get beyond the problem, and use your energy to make positive progress.

Cognitive Therapy

Cognitive therapy involves helping an individual modify and eventually reverse negative thought patterns. The belief is that depression is the consequence of an individual's negative thoughts about themselves, and the therapy puts your situation in a more positive light; you are better able to break out of your depression. On the other hand, I also believe that when you have bipolar disorder, depression can occur for absolutely no reason.

Changing Your Way of Thinking

Changing your way of thinking can help you to lead a better life. The following ideas can help not only those with bipolar disorder, but anyone who wants some improvement in her life. If you are unhappy, stressed out, or depressed most of the time, then it's time to retrain your brain to deal with your feelings and problems. It is not easy to make changes, but if you start now, in time, it will get better. The longer you think negatively, the longer it takes to make the change. If you had a heart condition or diabetes you would make the changes necessary to improve your physical health. It's the same with bipolar disorder. You have to change the way you live your life. You can take control. It all comes down to you.

Things Happen

When something bad happens to you, it can continue to take its toll long after the original damage has occurred. In the absence of anything else to focus on, you're likely to continue dwelling on it and allowing it to put a negative spin on everything in your life. Being bipolar is a challenge, and challenges are life's way of showing you that you can be stronger, more capable, more creative, and more highly focused than you ever thought possible. By thinking positively, you will gain added powers in fighting your illness. Even when the worst that could happen has indeed come to pass, in your thoughts, you can turn it around. Even if everything seems to be working against you, you can still think of ways to make it all work out.

Choose Your Thoughts

You can make the choice and make the effort to be happy. In your mind, you can go anywhere and do anything that you can imagine. You can find good things in everything you do. No circumstance can prevent you from choosing the thoughts you wish to choose. Your thoughts can take you anywhere you want to go. It's all about how you want to think about things. It is hard to make progress if you are hanging onto the things that are holding you back. Replace the negative thoughts and destructive habits with positive thinking and productive actions. Many times in my life, when I got stressed out or depressed, I would dwell on my problems. I couldn't sleep. I wouldn't eat right. My mind would take me back to my old negative ways of thinking. I call this the "snowball effect." I would find myself spiraling into the same pattern of negative thought, alcohol abuse, and thoughts of suicide. I tried self-talk. I would tell myself not to dwell on a problem, and to replace the negative thinking with positive thoughts. If I was thinking about suicide, I would say to myself, *Give it some more time, and see if things get better.* Ironically, the willingness to undertake the difficult task of getting well makes it easier to get well. I told myself to imagine how much smoother life would be if I could simply think more positively and put my best efforts into getting better.

10

Goals and Your Self-Esteem

When you are doing well, it helps to set goals for yourself, so when the bad times come, you can hang onto the goals. I tell myself that I have to live right now, because I have to get well and meet my goal. I've used writing this book as one of my goals. I also hang on for the next juggling show, or my next SHEP program. In the summer, my goal may be to make a garden and work in my yard. In the winter, I might fix up a room in the house. I write down what I want to do, and when the bad times come, I have something to work toward. I pick a goal from my list and get it done.

It's hard when you crash, but when you give your all, better things will come. Learn to take care of yourself first and make good choices. Stop and think about what you are about to do. Ask yourself, *Will I regret this choice later?*

Self-esteem affects how you think, act, and feel. Your level of self-esteem is determined by how you see yourself and the situation you're in. Because it affects your whole life, from the way you feel to how successful you are in achieving your goals, high self-esteem can make you feel effective, happy, productive, and loveable. Low self-esteem can make you feel unloved, worthless, unhappy, incompetent, and reluctant to try new things.

You can improve your self-esteem. Don't let past failures hold you back. You owe it to yourself to feel good about whom you are. Your life is filled with opportunities. Keep adding small positive changes to your life, and the results can be great.

Self-Esteem Test

Take this self-esteem test to see where you are. Answer YES or NO:

__Are you easily hurt by criticism?

__Are you shy, or overly aggressive?

__Do you try to hide your feelings from others?

__Do you fear close relationships?

__Do you try to blame your mistakes on others?

__Do you find excuses for refusing to change?

__Do you avoid new experiences?

__Do you continually wish you could change your physical appearance?

__Are you too modest about personal successes?

__Are you glad when others fail?

If you answered yes to most of the questions, your self-esteem could probably use improvement.

Answer YES or NO:

__Do you accept constructive criticism?

__Are you at ease when meeting new people?

__Are you honest and open about feelings?

__Do you value your closest relationships?

__Are you able to laugh at and learn from your own mistakes?

__Do you notice and accept changes in yourself as they occur

__Do you look for and tackle new challenges?

__Are you confident about your physical appearance?

__Do you give yourself credit where credit is due?

__Are you happy for others when they succeed?

If you answered yes to most of these questions, you probably have a healthy opinion of yourself. Even if you did not do well on this test, you can still change your self-esteem for the better. It's never too late. Think about the things you're proud of. Everyone has pride in something.

Setting Goals

The process of finding out what you want in your life is the first step in setting goals. What are your wants and needs? What is a realistic goal for you? Ask yourself these questions:

What do I love to do?
What am I good at?
What makes me happy?
What kind of job would I like?
What is realistic? What is unrealistic?
What will I be satisfied with?
How can I achieve my goal?
What problems do I have that will stop me from getting what I want?

Time to Set Your Goals

Start with a small goal, one you feel you can meet in a short period of time. When I was learning to juggle, I would set a goal every day to see how many throws I could get in the air before dropping a ball. I was so excited when I surpassed my record by ten throws. This small achievement really helped to raise my self-esteem.

Take on a larger goal, one that you can continue to work on over time. I decided to juggle for money. It took me a year or so before I was good enough, but by the age of thirteen, I was juggling at fairs all over the state, and making money doing what I loved.

I gave this speech at the end of each of the SHEP Programs:

> We can become just about anything we want in our free country, America. We have so many choices. Please take advantage of what choices you have. Work on your goal, whatever it may be. Set your goal today, and make it realistic. Start with a small goal, and when you meet it, go for the next one. As you meet each goal, your self-esteem will get higher and higher. Remember, you may have a setback, but don't quit. Give it your best try; that's all you can ask of yourself. Accept who you are and appreciate your own special talents. Make it a point to be your own best friend. Identify and accept your strengths and weaknesses. Take pride in your achievements, great and small. Accept and learn from your mistakes; this means accepting your failures as well as your successes. Be yourself.

Finding the Right Job for You

When you are ready to take charge of your life and you are feeling empowered, take time to evaluate your job. Are you happy where you work? I am asking this because a large part of your day is spent at your place of work. If you are bipolar and do not enjoy your job, it could be a contributing factor to your illness.

My dad wanted me to go to work in a factory, and I was going to do it. I knew I needed money. I was broke, and about to lose everything. I was doing better, but I was not sure if I was well enough to go to work every day. I had a fear of working at a job I didn't like, and it might cause me to go back into depression. I loved performing my juggling shows and writing prevention programs. At one point in my life, I was doing well being self-employed. The fact is that I never could hold a normal day job for too long. I needed adventure and a challenge. One day, I was looking over my old SHEP program. I was reminded of all I had accomplished and how I had done it all on my own. I had gained my knowledge from my experiences in life and from the books I had read. I began reading over my self-esteem program. I was amazed at what I read. I couldn't believe how I used to think. I was so positive and sure of myself, but I had changed for the worse and had forgotten my own teachings. But now I began to see the ways in which I could make a positive difference. I found that the more time I spent each day being the person I truly was, the faster I moved forward.

This is what I had written on the back of my self-esteem booklets:

> Self-esteem is the answer to feeling better about who we are. Self-esteem can help us, because we all know life is not fair or easy. We all have to work to get where we want to go in life. We must deal with many setbacks; sometimes there seems to be no light at the end of the tunnel, but do not quit. Think of the good things. We all need to feel loved. We all need a purpose in life. Don't let past failures hold you back. Start your day with a strong belief in yourself. If you don't believe in yourself, who will?

11

Keep Your Mind and Body Healthy

To maintain a healthy mind and body, changes may be necessary. I have made some important ones over the past five years.

The following is an outline of my exercise:

Keep this in mind: too much of anything is not a good thing. Use and do things in moderation.

Exercise

I exercise at least three times a week, just a fifteen-to-thirty-minute workout. When working in my office all day, I take time to stretch or go for a walk to make me feel better.

Caffeine

Use it in moderation. Like most people, I used to believe that I needed coffee to get me going in the morning. I used to drink two pots of coffee a day and drink Mountain Dew all day long. I never thought I would give it up. I did an experiment for one month: I gave up all caffeine, replacing it with a multivitamin and food. I felt so much better. I had no more headaches, and my stomach no longer hurt. Now I have real energy—not artificially induced energy.

Alcohol Use in Moderation

I no longer drink alcohol. There was a time when I was drinking almost every day for one month. I kept close notes on how I was doing, and filled out my symptom chart every day, recording how I felt, what it did to me, and how it affected my bipolar symptoms:

1. I got a lot less done in a day.

2. I felt sick most of the day.

3. I did not eat right, and I felt very weak.

4. I woke up often at night and had dreams that felt real.

5. I got depressed.

6. I was very suicidal.

7. I experienced memory loss.

8. I made bad choices.

About four weeks into my drinking, I became very sick. I was not eating right, and I was taking my medication with alcohol. This made the lithium go to toxic levels in my blood. The next thing I knew, I was in an ambulance, going to the hospital. The doctor told me I could have died.

I came home from the hospital and was still very sick and depressed. I was cold and could not get warm. After seven days, I still could not eat or sleep. I was so weak and sick that I could not stop shaking.

I went to Dr. Turkin and asked him to admit me to the adult unit, where I received vitamins and the help I needed. When I went over my charts later, I could clearly see the bad effects alcohol had had on me. However, I did mess up Again about ten months ago, I had a few bad days and was feeling depressed. I was thinking about drinking. I ended up drunk and eventually I passed out, only to wake up in my own vomit. I had one hell of a headache. I looked at my arm and saw that I had cut myself. I didn't even remember doing it. I felt guilty for letting myself get to that point; I was upset with myself for screwing up. Drinking did not make anything any better. If anything, it made it worse. My therapist, Mark, told me to just move forward; it was okay. I messed up, but I didn't need to keep punishing myself. So I forgave myself and told myself I was going to quit drinking, and here I am, ten months later, sober and feeling good.

Eat Right

I take a multivitamin every day. I eat every morning, even if it's just some toast and a glass of milk. It is very important to keep your body well-nourished. Try it for a week, and you will feel better and have more energy.

I Talk to My Friends

Let your friends help you. Sometimes they can see the problem before you do. I have a good friend named Robby at the fire hall, and he knows everything about me. He can tell when I'm not doing well. He listens to me without judgment, and helps when he can.

Take Time for Family and Friends (You Need Them)

My daughters and I go out to a restaurant or for ice cream once a week. I take time to do things with my family.

I try to get over to my best friend Karen's house once a week, or at least talk on the phone with her. She is a good friend. She would drop everything to help me if I needed her. I once was hospitalized for being depressed. Prior to this, I had pushed everyone away. When I was ready to be discharged from the hospital, I did not have a ride home. I called Karen, with whom I had not spoken to in six months. She dropped everything to come get me. A good friend like Karen is someone you want to have around.

What I am saying is that whatever state of bipolar disorder you're in; do not shut out your family and friends.

Take the Time to Enjoy Life

Take a break and have some fun. I do things I love to do, like camping and fishing with friends.

Sleep

When manic, be sure to get your sleep every night. Without it, you will end up falling into depression. Get your sleep, and make up for any lost sleep. Before, I would just keep going, and the less sleep I got, the more depressed I became.

If you have trouble sleeping, ask your doctor to give you sleeping pills for a week or so until you are back on track. Even if I am out on a fire call all night, I make sure to make up my sleep as soon as I can.

Take Your Medication as Prescribed.

Work with your doctor to ensure that you are taking the right medications in the right amounts.

Keep Your Appointments.

This is part of your get-well plan. It is important to stick with it. If you have to miss an appointment, make it up as soon as possible. My life is scheduled around my appointments.

When You Are Suicidal or Depressed,

It is important to have a plan ready that you can put into effect. I have all my emergency numbers with me at all times, so I can call someone if I start feeling too bad. Make all weapons unavailable. I took my hunting guns to a friend's house, and he won't give them back unless he knows I'm okay.

As for Where I Am Now

I started writing this book while I was still on my roller coaster of mood swings. I was hoping that the ending would be a happy one, and I am glad to say that I have achieved my goal. I have finished writing this book, and I have a happy ending. I am doing very well. I still participate in two bipolar research programs to better my life. I am a volunteer firefighter with the Penfield Volunteer Fire Department (Station 41)

I am now self-employed doing what I love: the SHEP programs and my juggling. I am working on new skills and have learned many new things. I wake up each morning and tell myself what a beautiful day it is to be alive. I look around and see the beauty in everything. I am happy and thankful for all that I have.

A desire to get better, medication, talk therapy, and my symptom charts got me to where I am right now. I must say that at first, I didn't like not being manic; but as I got used to it and settled down into my new lifestyle, I found I could enjoy things more. Now I can get involved in a project and actually stop and take a break. I get tired at night. I can fall asleep and sleep all night. I love life right now. I spend time with my kids, I have fun, and I am doing the things I love to do. My sixteen-year-old daughter, Jessica, is still living with me and doing very well. My nineteen-year-old daughter, Sheena, is studying to be a psychologist. I am so proud of her.

Conclusion

I will leave you with these thoughts. There is nothing to be gained by wishing that things had been different. Instead, put your energy into living. Take advantage of the countless possibilities that are now in front of you. Even small changes can have a positive impact on you. It's up to you how you want to live your life. Make the right choices, and be positive. Work for a better future for yourself. Nothing happens overnight. It took me five years to get this far, and I now feel more normal that I ever did in my life. I am neither manic nor depressed. With this book and my get-well plan, I am hoping it won't be long before you are feeling your very best. I am not saying you will not have the ups and downs anymore. The idea here is to help make them less frequent and less severe, so you can live your life better.

About My Mom Christine

Christine is my mom, and I am very proud of her. She has come a long way. Through her book, I have been better able to understand her illness. I only wish I'd had this book years ago, so I could have understood what was wrong with my mom back then. I hope you get as much out of this book as I have since she has been using her charting system and has learned to cut back on her activities, Mom is doing much better. Sometimes I even see her turning to her own book for advice on what to do, or to remind herself what she should be doing. My mom is a very caring person who has a passion to help make a difference in people's lives…

If you want to meet my mom you can find her in some peculiar places. Year-round, you may see her in Clearfield County or Elk County, Pennsylvania, out along the roadway with the fire department at an accident site, doing what she loves to do: helping people in need. Wintertime she spends traveling, doing her SHEP Programs or juggling shows. In spring-time, you may find her in Jones Township, Pennsylvania, at East Branch Dam, operating a backhoe or heavy equipment on a private road called Maple Lain, which she maintains. In summertime, mom is out and about, doing juggling shows. When she has a break, she enjoys camping at East Branch Dam. She loves the outdoors. It relaxes her. It's a chance for her to do her own thing. In the fall, when archery season comes in, you will only find her in the woods, hunting deer. She will leave in the early morning to go out into the woods, and only comes out after dark. She is a dedicated hunter.

—Sheena Stefano

This book is a product of the SHEP Programs
Self-Help Educational Prevention-Ed Programs
Providing self-help educational services since 1995

The SHEP Programs were developed by Christine, who has experience as a domestic-violence counselor, child advocate, sexual-assault counselor, and prevention-ed coordinator. Christine wrote and presented many of her programs in schools throughout the USA. She also starred in her own children's video called "What About Self-Esteem and Setting Goals?" Christine has been a professional juggler, puppeteer, and ventriloquist since 1982.

SHEP Programs

Juggling Show with a Special Message
Teen Dating Danger
What About Self-Esteem?
Hands Are Not for Hitting
About Bullies, Friends, and More
Better Kid Care Program
Juggling Your Bipolar Life

APPENDIX

Making a Symptom Chart Checklist

This is an example of how to create and fill out your personalized medication checklist:

This is just an example. You should add or delete options based on your needs.

It is important to keep track of all the medications you are taking. This helps to track if there are any reactions between them. Also note if you have a mood change while taking that medication.

When making your chart, be sure to make extra blank spaces for use if you get prescribed new medications or other variables come into play, such as cold medication, pain pills, antibiotics, etc., so you can write them in as well. Also be sure to note any as needed, or "rescue medications" that you may be prescribed. Their use is also important to note, their frequency and duration.

First make your chart. I like to use the first column to list my medications. I also like to use one column for each day, using the same chart for an entire week. You can certainly use a daily chart or a monthly chart, but for me, the weekly method seems to work best.

Next, write the date at the top of the chart.

Then fill in the weight you are for the first day of the week.

At the top of the chart write in next to the day of the week the date for each day...

Use the first column of the chart for what medications you are taking, how many milligrams that you take daily, and the time you take it.

Now it is time to keep track of your medications. Be honest. If you miss a dose, leave it blank. If you take more or less, write that in also. Consistency is important. Without detailed and accurate information, you will not be able to accurately track symptoms, hindering your results.

Be sure to keep a list of side effects you may be experiencing and share them with your doctor as soon as possible.

Date 1/2/2006   Weight 140

Medication	mg	Time	Mon 2 Time	Mg	mg	Tues Time	mg	Wed Time	mg	Thurs Time	mg	Fri Time	mg	Sat Time	mg	Sun Time	mg
Tylenol	675	9 Pm	9 pm	675	675	10 PM	675										
Seroquel	400	9 Pm	9 pm	400	200	10pm	200										
Other																	
Tylenol	300	7am	7am	300													
Pain pill																	
Seroquel	25	7am	7am	25													
Vitamin		7am	7am														

How to Put Your Symptom Chart All Together

How to put your chart together

This is a sample symptom checklist chart for you to use to start your own.
Write the date in, then write the dates over the days of the week.
Fill in your weigh for the first day of the week.

Date: _____ Weight:	8th Monday	9th Tuesday	10th Wednesday	11th Thursday	12th Friday	13th Saturday	14th Sunday
As for women: Your menstrual cycle may play a part in your mood swing and you may fall into depression easily. It is something to watch for so as you could be prepared for it.							
Do you have your menstrual cycle							

Notes:

Sometimes I write notes on my chart to let me know more of what is going on at that time.
This helps me know why I may have felt the way I did at that time, for exempla was it just my bipolar, or was it from a stresor in my life that made me feel like I did.

Notes							
Stresor of the day							

When you make your own chart you can fill in the symptoms that you feel you are having.

Then you can see if it is a symptom of bipolar or if it is a stressor of yours.

For the first few months you may need to add symptoms as they occur, so be sure to leave some blank spaces to add your new symptoms.

For the symptom checklist chart, I use the following system:

I put an XX after the question if I feel strongly about how I feel.

If I am feeling somewhat bad or good, I just use an X.

If I do not feel all that bad or good, I put a / or leave it blank.

Put your x in the box of the time of day your symptom occurs AM, N or PM

Manic	Am	N	Pm

Date___ Weight	8th Monday Am	N	Pm	9th Tuesday Am	N	Pm	10th Wednesday Am	N	Pm	11th Thursday Am	N	Pm	12th Friday Am	N	Pm	13th Saturday Am	N	Pm	14th Sunday Am	N	Pm
Do you feel Manic				X	X	X															
Racing thoughts						XX	XX														
Elated mood					X	X															
Rapid speech																					
Bursts of energy						X		X													
Less need for sleep						X	X														
Irritability																					

Date ___ Weight ___	Monday			Tuesday			Wednesday			Thursday			Friday			Saturday			Sunday		
Depressed	Am	N	Pm	Am	N	Pm	Am	N	Pm	Am	N	Pm	Am	N	Pm	Am	N	Pm	Am	N	Pm
Do you feel Depressed		X	XX																		
Memory loss																					
Negative		X	XX																		
Paranoid			X																		
Anxiety		X	XX																		
Cry a lot		X	XX																		
Very jumpy																					
Sensitive to noise																					
Feel like you want to run away																					
Cannot feel happy			X																		
Lack of motivation			X																		
Stay in bed																					
Want to do self harm			XX																		
Did you hurt yourself																					

	8th Monday Am	N	Pm	9th Tuesday Am	N	Pm	10th Wednesday Am	N	Pm	11th Thursday Am	N	Pm	12th Friday Am	N	Pm	13th Saturday Am	N	Pm	14th Sunday Am	N	Pm
Date ___ Weight ___																					
Suicidal		X	XX																		
Do not care about anything		X	X																		
Thinking about dying		X	XX																		
Want to die		X	XX																		
Making plans to kill yourself			X																		
Have the things to kill yourself			X																		

CALL FOR HELP NOW IF YOU FELL THIS WAY!

Your sleep habits play a large part in helping to show if you are depressed or manic.
*Write the time in the **Pm** or **Am** box what time you went to bed.*
*Then write in the **Am** or **Pm** box what time you woke up.*
Next write in the hours of sleep you got that night.
Then mark an X if you took a nap or stayed in bed all day.

Date _____ Weight _____	Monday			Tuesday			Wednesday			Thursday			Friday			Saturday			Sunday		
Sleep habits	Am	N	Pm	Am	N	Pm	Am	N	Pm	Am	N	Pm	Am	N	Pm	Am	N	Pm	Am	N	Pm
Time went to sleep			10																		
Time woke up	8																				
Hours slept	8 Hours																				
Hard to fall asleep			X																		
Woke up often			X																		
Sleep all day																					
Did you take a nap		X																			
Laid in bed awake		X																			

Appetite increase or decrease and /or abdominal problems may be related to your medication, Bipolar illness or a stressor in your life.

Date ____ Weight ____	Monday			Tuesday			Wednesday			Thursday			Friday			Saturday			Sunday		
	AM	N	PM	AM	N	PM	AM	N	PM	AM	N	PM	AM	N	PM	AM	N	PM	AM	N	PM
Eating habits																					
Decrease of appetite	X		X																		
Loss of appetite	X		X																		
Increase of appetite																					
Forget to eat																					
Abdominal problems																					
Nausea			X																		
Vomiting																					
Diarrhea																					
Constipation			X																		

Substance use: *This will help you see how caffeine, alcohol or drugs use can affect your bipolar illness.*
Write the number of caffeine or alcohol drinks you had that day.
If you have any other addictions you may make a chart for them as well.

Substance use	Am	N	Pm	Am	N	Pm	Am	N	Pm	Am	N	Pm	Am	N	Pm	Am	N	Pm	Am	N	Pm
Caffeine drinks	2	1	1																		
alcohol																					
Number of drinks			X																		
feel like you needed to be drunk or high			X																		
Feel like you need to stop the pain			X																		
Did you get drunk or high			X																		
How many cigarettes did you smoke	2	6	5																		
Did you smoke more			X																		

Sex drive

This is just for you to keep track of your own actions
The sex drive part is to help you to see if you are being promiscuous.
This is something people with bipolar illness need to watch out for.
If you know what is going on you can try to prevent it and possible save your relationship with your significant other.
Plus prevent an unwanted pregnancy or contracting STD.

Date____ Weight____	Monday			Tuesday			Wednesday			Thursday			Friday			Saturday			Sunday		
Sex drive	Am	N	Pm	Am	N	Pm	Am	N	Pm	Am	N	Pm	Am	N	Pm	Am	N	Pm	Am	N	Pm
Increased sex drive																					
Decreases sex drive																					
Promiscuity																					
Flirtatious																					
Did you have sex																					
With whom																					

Christine's Symptom Chart Checklist

Christine's symptom checklist chart

This is an example of one of the charts I completed while monitoring my symptoms. As you look at my weekly symptom chart, you can see that I went from manic to depressed to suicidal in a week's time. This is a true copy of my weekly symptom chart from March 2003. Back in March, after looking at my chart and seeing how bad I truly was feeling, I called my doctor and admitted myself to the adult behavioral health unit. I stayed until the suicidal thoughts passed. Remember, it is better to be safe than sorry. Get help when you need it.

Weight 138 Date 2003	10 Monday			11 Tuesday			12 Wednesday			13 Thursday			14 Friday			15 Saturday			16 Sunday		
	Am	N	Pm	Am	N	Pm	Am	N	Pm	Am	N	Pm	Am	N	Pm	Am	N	Pm	Am	N	Pm
Menstrual cycle	yes			yes																	
Stressor	Money			Juggling shows									Money			Kids/house					
Notes:																Bad day			Bad day		
Manic																					
Are you manic?	X	x	x	x	x	x	x	xx	x	x						x	x				
Racing thoughts	x	x	x	x	x	x	x	xx	x	x						x	x				
Hyperactive	x	x	x	x	x	x	x	xx	xx												
Elated mood	x	x	x	x		x	x	x	xx												
Rapid speech							x	x	xx												
Bursts of energy	x	x	x	x	x	x	x	x	x												
Need less sleep	x	x	x	x	x	x	x	x	x												

Weight 138 Date 2003	10 Monday	11 Tuesday	12 Wednesday	13 Thursday	14 Friday	15 Saturday	16 Sunday
Depressed					x x	x	xx xx xxx
Do you feel depressed?					x x	x x	xx xx xx
Difficulty concentrating						x	x x x
Irritability						x	xx x x
Forget full						x	xx xx x
Memory loss						x	xx x x
Paranoid					x x	x	xx xx x
Cry a lot						x	xx xx x
Anxiety						x	xx xx x
Very jumpy						x x	x x x
Sensitive to noise						x	x x x
Feel like you want to run away						x	
Cant feel happy							x x x
Want to cut							xx xx xx
Want to hurt yourself							x x x
Did you harm yourself?							
Feel negative							x xx

Suicidal
- Do not care about anything
- Thinking about dying
- Want to die
- Making plans to kill yourself
- Have the stuff to kill your self

Eating habits
- Loss of appetite
- Forget to eat

Abdominal pain
- Nausea
- Vomiting
- Diarrhea
- Constipation

Substance use
- Caffeine drink k
- How much alcohol?
- Did you feel like you needed to be drunk or high?
- Feel like you needed to stop the pain
- Did you get drunk or high?
- How many cigarettes did you smoke?
- Did you smoke more?

Date 2003 Weight 138	Monday			Tuesday			Wednesday			Thursday			Friday			Saturday			Sunday		
	Am	N	Pm	Am	N	Pm	Am	N	Pm	Am	N	Pm	Am	N	Pm	Am	N	Pm	Am	N	Pm
Sex Drive																					
Increased sex drive	/	/	/	/	/	/	X				X	X	X	X	X	X		X	X	X	X
Decreased sex drive									X												
Promiscuity												X			X			X			X
Flirtatious												X			X			X			X
Did you have sex												X									X
With whom												?									?
Sleep habits																					
Time went to sleep	12			2					11	2					10			11	10		11
Time woke up	5			5			7			5			7			7			10		
Hours slept	5			3			8			3			9			8			12		
Took a nap																					
Laid in bed awake			x			x			x			x							x		
Hard to fall asleep									x			x								x	
Woke up often									x			x									
Dreams feel real									x			x									x

Simple Symptom Chart Checklist

Simple symptom chart
You may use this chart when you are feeling better and have a better grasp of your symptom.

	Monday AM	N	PM	Tuesday AM	N	PM	Wednesday AM	N	PM	Thursday AM	N	PM	Friday AM	N	PM	Saturday AM	N	PM	Sunday AM	N	PM
Date___ Weight___																					
Menstrual cycle																					
Stressor of the day																					
Notes																					
Manic																					
Stable																					
Mild																					
Moderate																					
Severe																					
Depressed																					
Stable																					
Mild																					
Moderate																					
Severe																					
Suicidal																					
Stable																					
Mild																					
Moderate																					
Severe																					
Stressed out																					
Stable																					
Mild																					
Moderate																					
Severe																					

978-0-595-37771-8
0-595-37771-8

www.ingramcontent.com/pod-product-compliance
Lightning Source LLC
Chambersburg PA
CBHW080418290526
45791CB00008BA/2321